guiding
a church school

WALTER TOWNER

𝒜abingdon

press / new york · nashville

GUIDING A CHURCH SCHOOL

Library of Congress Catalog Card Number: 63-19032

SET UP, PRINTED AND BOUND BY THE
PARTHENON PRESS, AT NASHVILLE,
TENNESSEE, UNITED STATES OF AMERICA

To RUTH my wife

whose love, loyalty,
wise counsel, and Christian
courage have inspired me
through the years

preface

Two factors combined to call this book into existence. One cannot for many years travel the length and breadth of the nation and have firsthand contact with local church schools without knowing that their leaders want help. In the process the traveler learns much from those who are succeeding—and from those who are failing. It seems desirable to try to make the accumulated information available as one more source of help for the Christian men and women who guide our church schools.

In the book are ideas and in some instances the exact wording used by this writer in pamphlets and articles he has written for his church through the years. In the section on age grouping, where the ideas are common to most denominations, some of the brief explanations are taken from board guidance pamphlets, and I have made no effort to put them in my own words. The indulgence of my church is hopefully assumed.

There is a sense in which it is futile to write a book on guiding the present church school. The book is out of date before it can be printed. Procedures are changing rapidly, but that is not why. The reason is that the rethinking of the nature of the church and its ministry and of education is bringing about changes that will put the teaching work of the church in new perspective and new context. So why bother to help guide the present church school? My answer is that some of the new is reflected. Also, it will be years before practice in the local church can catch up with emerging theory even after it has been tested. Let's go ahead and do the best we can with what we have. I hope that is a good enough answer to justify this kind of book.

I want to thank four of the finest Christians I know—Randle Dew, Ernest Dixon, Glenn Gothard, and Wayne Lindecker—men with whom I am associated in the Department of General Church School Work of The Methodist Church. They took seriously my request that they focus their wide knowledge of the local church school on the manuscript. They did a thorough job of exposing inadequacies for rewriting. That the book is not better is not their fault.

And I heartily thank Mary Hall for the service in preparing the manuscript which could be rendered only by a loyal and extremely competent secretary.

—WALTER TOWNER

1

THE KIND OF BOOK THIS IS

What We Are Undertaking

This is a book about how to guide a church school. It undertakes to present practical solutions for many of the common, and some of the uncommon, problems which arise. It is for workers who are looking for help in handling their jobs.

This is not a book about theology or educational philosophy or even about how to teach. There are many good books about these things. Church-school workers certainly should read them. But in those portions which have relationship to these fields, this book undertakes to be in harmony with Protestant theology and good educational theory and with modern teaching procedures. If the book wanders from the narrow path it undertakes to travel, the reader's Christian charity is enjoined.

Quite understandably, various denominations use different terms for essentially the same things. To avoid confusion, the nomenclature and practice of one denomination (Methodist) have been used throughout this book. For readers from other denominations substitution of their terms can easily be made. The following explanation of terms that will be encountered frequently may help in this:

Quarterly conference—The basic governing body of the local church.
Official board—The administrative body for the local church. It puts into effect the actions of the quarterly conference.
Commission on education—Analogous to committee on or board of education. References will be encountered to commissions in other fields such as missions, stewardship, and the like.
Workers' conference—The meeting of all teachers and officers in the church school.

Before getting into the heart of this book, note the statements which follow. They show the direction in which we are headed.

Christ-Centeredness

Much thought is being given these days to what the nature and mission of the church are. That is good. It is not contemplated, however, that action based on accepted goals will be halted until better ones emerge. The church, and therefore the church school, has always had a clear goal. It is to guide persons everywhere to know and accept Jesus Christ as Savior and Lord through meeting the conditions involved, to serve him and their fellowmen in the fellowship of his holy church, to bring others into that fellowship, and to live as Christians every day with emphasis on growing into the full richness that involves. The church (and hence its church school) is God's agency to redeem men and society.

It is the point of view of this book that a church school should have this clear focus.

Basic Dependence

Guiding a church school is a complex and difficult undertaking. Confidence that it can be done and clarity as to how it may be done will be aided by understanding three basic requirements:

1. "Not by might nor by power, but by my spirit, saith the Lord" is our first guidepost along the road to understanding how to guide a church school. The often stated direction "Work as though it all depends on you and pray as though it all depends on God," is a faulty admonition. The two are not separate concepts. It is more accurate to think of

12

working in the light of our dependence on God. The whole enterprise must go forward in the strength and under the guidance of the Holy Spirit.

2. Those who bear responsibility must be expendable. Quoting the words "Without shedding of blood [there] is no remission [of sins]" is often an invitation to theological disagreement. But there can be no disagreement over the fact that a price is to be paid for success in guiding a church school. It is a business costly to individual persons in time and energy and often in sacrifice.

3. Modern studies in leadership have emphasized a long known truth and have given us a term for it, the necessity for a "concerned group." It will be pointed out in this book that a brilliant leader working alone may fail where a group of normally capable persons praying and working together will succeed. The church-school administrator who makes and executes the decisions seldom sees them bear good fruit.

Zeal

We are in the midst of revolution. Americans know that is true in the rest of the world, but we inadequately realize how true it is at home. We would be amazed if we could sense all the changes going on around us. What worked a decade, or less, ago may not work now. We must be willing to try new things. But in the midst of change we must continue to see clearly goals that do not change, be loyal to them, and work hard to reach them.

Zeal is often scoffed at. But earnest enthusiasm should characterize those who guide a church school. For reasons like these:

1. Anti-Christian forces have never been so powerful or so successful. At best military might and economic superiority can buy us only a little more time. The world deserves an opportunity to be Christian. And the only thing that really can save what is worthy in our Western world is true Christianity—the thing for which the church school exists.

2. Here in America, and to an extent even in our churches, true Christianity is sometimes hard to find. There is an appalling similarity between many inside the church and those outside the church. Many analysts are saying that at the very time when more persons are related to churches than ever before, the influence of the church in America is on the decline. But we believe in the church.

We believe in the church school. Despite all its faults it does a tremendous amount of good. It is an important factor in Christianizing the world even under discouraging modern conditions. Therefore, zeal is commended to those who guide a church school. The approach of this book is that it makes a difference whether people follow Christ. We are in a life and death struggle both for the souls of men and for the preservation of what is good in our society. While earnestness alone is not enough, those who guide church schools carry a heavy responsibility to be tremendously in earnest.

It is shortsighted to proceed as though things were automatically coming our way and all that we have to do is to improve here and there. Actually, our culture is showing an alarming disinterest in what we have to offer. But we must be prepared to work hard and with enthusiasm if we are to make progress.

Unity

Some think of the church as a bundle of organizations, one of which is the church school. Not so. The church should be one, expressing itself through various parts. The church school has an organization in order to get its work done, but is not itself primarily an organization. It has no independent existence. It is part of a whole, which is the church. The church school is the church engaged in teaching.

This oneness can be illustrated:

Christ indicated that his gospel should be taken to all the world. He made plain three ways to do it—teaching (Matt. 28:19-20), preaching (Matt. 10:5-7), and witnessing (Acts 1:8). As his followers did these three things, the church developed.

These three have been the business of the church ever since. Along with preaching and witnessing, teaching is at the heart of the work of the church by indication of the Founder of the church.

Unity should also characterize the way we go about the teaching work of the church. That brings us to an old question: Does the church do all its teaching through the church school? The answer is no if we are thinking about the kind of teaching which, for instance, the pastor does in his sermon. But the answer should be yes if we are thinking about teaching which follows a curriculum, is organized into classes and groups, and undertakes an orderly approach. A properly conducted church does this work through its church school. If our definition of the church school as the church engaged in teaching is accepted, this conclusion is inevitable.

But this statement needs exploring. Within the teaching program of the church there can be a unified approach or a multiple approach. Unified teaching is planned so the results fit together. There is a central agency (commission on education) which can insure that the teaching is not a conglomerate of unrelated parts, with overlappings and omissions, but instead is a unified whole. The opposite of this is a multiple approach. It is not centrally planned. Various groups in the church undertake to teach the same persons at such times as they can, with no relationships in what they are doing. For example, young people taught in a Sunday school, then in a Sunday evening youth group, and then in a weekday group—all separate organizations which have no planned and supervised relationship to one another. Unity can be achieved if Sunday morning, Sunday evening, and weekday are all under one total plan.

Nature

Those who guide the church school should understand the nature of the enterprise they are conducting.

As considered in the church school, Christian education is guidance. It is procedure. It is important that this be made clear.

It becomes clear when we think of education as teaching, including arranging situations for growth through the effect persons can have on one another. It can hardly be established that the total significance of education is contained within teaching, narrowly conceived. But in the realm of the church school, which is the context of this book, by Christian education we do mean Christian teaching in the broader sense.

If asked what the program of the church is, that is, what the church is trying to get done, a frequent answer is evangelism, education, missions, stewardship, and Christian social concerns. In such thinking there is a fundamental error. The error is in classification.

The five mentioned above are not co-ordinate parts which together compose a program. One of the five, education, is of a different order from the other four, if we equate education with teaching, as above. Teaching is a procedure to accomplish the other four, and to accomplish something else not necessarily encompassed by the other four—namely, Christian nurture and Christian knowledge which includes the Bible.

To understand the nature of the church school and its broad teaching program, one must think of it as a servant. It exists to accomplish things which are vital in the Christian program. One does not teach for teaching's sake. One teaches to evangelize, to develop missionary-mindedness, to encourage stewardship ideals and practices, to make real Christian social concerns and action, to nurture Christian growth and appropriation of Christian knowledge.

It is important to sort things out so they fall into place and the whole can be understood. Summarizing the above, we classify evangelism

15

(thought of here as commitment to Christ and church membership and to the Christian life), missions, stewardship, Christian social concerns, and Christian nurture and acquisition of Christian knowledge as things that must be done. And they are to be done by employing the New Testament procedures of preaching, teaching, and witnessing. (Parenthetically, it is to be noted that the three often overlap and frequently merge. It is unrealistic to try sharply to distinguish between them.) The church school must be at work in the whole of the Father's business. Just as preaching concerns itself with all of it, so must teaching.

In this connection it is interesting to note that Bishop W. C. Martin, in the Episcopal Address to the 1960 Methodist General Conference, said:

> Let us consider the ministry. . . . Is it not a justifiable expectancy that there will come, each year, from our seminaries a stream of graduates who, with deep appreciation of . . . Biblical and doctrinal scholarship and of liturgical skill, are fully aware that these are means to an end; . . . men who understand Christ's command to preach, to teach, and to witness, and who will be skilled in all three?

Product

What can be said about the product of the church school?

Quite definitely the work of the church school should produce something. So it is accurate to think of the part of the church which we call the church school as producing something. What should it be?

We will not find the answer by trying to isolate the church school. The answer must be in terms of the oneness of the church of which the church school is a part. Some of us do not feel that the answer will be found in statements of "goals of Christian education," as though Christian education had goals apart from the goals of the church. The purpose of the church school is identical with the purpose of the church, within the general scope of the teaching procedure.

The product for which we work is lives changed toward Christ, lives committed to Christ's Lordship and Saviorhood and basically oriented in and successfully practicing the Christian way. A teacher has accomplished the purposes of Christian teaching when there is such a product.

Here, again, we have come to something that is so important that it should be clearly understood.

Erroneously, some think that the purpose of Christian teaching is accomplished when knowledge about holy things has been imparted by a teacher to those being taught. Those who feel this way would illustrate by saying that when knowledge of the Bible has been imparted, the

16

goal of Christian teaching has been reached. Thus our product would be persons informed about the contents of the Bible.

But the Bible record of what the Master Teacher taught gives no support to such an idea. That for which he died, arose, and continues to live is persons. Our product should be a kind of person. The full richness of what is meant cannot be stated in the brief compass appropriate here. But the heart of the idea is this: persons informed and committed to Christ and his church in the fullest, richest sense who are continuing to grow in understanding and in living his way.

The product for which we work is Christian disciples. But what is meant by Christian discipleship?

I was asked that question in a meeting of church-school leaders. In substance this was the reply: "Is this not representative of our highest ideals, that Christian discipleship means

—complete, absolute commitment to Jesus Christ as Lord, Master, and Savior as a living person and constant companion;
—yielding to God's purposes as revealed in Christ all that one is and all that one has, without reservation;
—maintenance of a deep and lasting purpose to grow in the understanding and the practice of God's will for one's life, and the richness of one's worship and prayer;
—service to one's fellowmen as Christ's ambassador, putting the welfare of others above one's own;
—diligent and continuing effort to guide others into Christian discipleship and the church, in which one serves loyally and joyously?"

But how would you state it? Differently, no doubt. Yet, however it is stated, in its truest and most Christian form it describes what the church school is trying to bring about in human lives. This is our desired product.

To be sure, on the way to the goal vast attention must be given to helping persons achieve knowledge of the Bible, the church, and the whole range of sacred information. This is necessary. But this is not the goal of the church. It simply is a necessary achievement on the way to the goal.

Those who guide a church school should have a clear understanding of what its product should be. Many teachers do not understand. They think they have accomplished the purpose of Christian teaching when those they have taught are able to answer questions accurately, evidencing a good store of knowledge about holy things.

Unfortunately, there is no *necessary* correlation between what a per-

17

son knows and what he does. Our product must be on a level higher than just information.

The Rest of This Book

The remainder of this book deals with proposed solutions for problems which face persons who guide a church school. These problems have been voiced by hundreds of groups of church-school administrators throughout the nation. And in discussing them we will, as often as possible, search for guiding principles, the neglect of which caused the problems. It is hoped that what is offered will be help toward solutions.

2

PROVIDING LEADERS

The question most frequently asked in groups of church-school administrators is, "How do you get teachers?" The question can be answered, but the answer is not a simple one. This chapter attempts to answer it.

Here is a general outline for an answer:
1. Understand what "leader" in church school means.
2. Fix wisely responsibility for providing leaders.
3. Have a plan and follow it.

Understanding What "Leader" Means

We know that in a class which is doing good work, from time to time different members function in a leadership capacity in one way or another, except with very small children. So the dividing line between teacher and member becomes dim at times. Nevertheless we recognize the need for persons to carry particular responsibilities. In almost all classes we do have persons who serve as teachers. By "leaders" in the church school we mean those persons, preferably changing from time to time, who carry responsibility in some specialized way for the Christian progress of others.

One Christian educator stated it this way: "Leadership is a shared function, but within the sharing group some persons have specific functions to carry out. We refer to these persons as leaders, but that does not relieve members of the class or group from their leadership responsibility."

Increasingly we recognize the values in "limited tenure" for teachers and other leaders and for rotation in office. Therefore, it seems wise to say that although we are searching for leaders, we are not expecting to set them apart permanently as "our leaders."

It is likewise of basic importance that serving as a leader should stem from discipleship. This is discussed later.

Fixing Responsibility for Providing Leaders

In American denominations there is wide variation in procedure for securing church-school leaders. And there is variation between churches within a denomination. In deciding who is responsible for securing leaders the local church school should know the pattern provided by its own denomination. To illustrate the detail involved in fixing responsibility clearly, the procedure in one denomination (Methodist) is stated below:

In this denomination responsibility for providing a leadership in the church school rests partly with the quarterly conference, partly with the commission on education, and partly with the class or group (youth and adult divisions). The following is taken from the Methodist *Discipline:*

¶ 246. Great care shall be exercised in the selection of teachers, officers, and other workers in the church school. They shall be elected annually in the following manner:

1. The Quarterly Conference shall elect, to serve from the beginning of the ensuing conference or church-school year: (*a*) the church-school superintendent; (*b*) a membership cultivation superintendent and three division superintendents; (*c*) a director of Christian education, or educational assistant, if

desired. Interim vacancies shall be filled by the Commission on Education, the pastor concurring, subject to confirmation by the next Quarterly Conference.

2. Each class or group concerned shall elect, prior to the beginning of the church-school year or as need may arise: (a) youth officers in the Youth Division; (b) officers in the Adult Division; and (c) the teachers of adult classes, after consultation with the church-school superintendent. Teachers of adult classes shall be subject to confirmation by the Commission on Education.

3. The Commission on Education shall elect, prior to the beginning of the church-school year, all teachers, officers, and workers not otherwise provided for, on nomination of the church-school superintendent with the approval of the pastor, the minister or director of Christian education, and the division superintendents.

¶ 247. 1. On nomination of the pastor, with the concurrence of the Commission on Education and the Committee on Pastoral Relations or the Committee on Lay Personnel, the Quarterly Conference may annually request the bishop to appoint, or may employ, a minister or director of Christian education or an educational assistant, who in co-operation with the pastor and the church-school superintendent shall guide the educational program of the local church in accordance with ¶ 233 and with the standards of the General Board of Education. He shall be administratively responsible to the pastor. Provided he is certified as described in ¶ 1451, his title shall be minister of Christian education if he is an ordained ministerial member of an Annual Conference, or director of Christian education if he is a layman. In case he is not certified, his title shall be educational assistant. Two or more churches may join in using the services of such a person.

2. On nomination of the pastor, with the concurrence of the Music Committee, the Commission on Education, and the Committee on Pastoral Relations or the Committee on Lay Personnel, the Quarterly Conference may annually request the bishop to appoint, or may employ, a minister or director of music, who shall direct the total music program of the local church in accordance with the standards of the General Board of Education and of the General Commission on Worship. He shall be administratively responsible to the pastor. Provided he is certified as described in ¶ 1451, his title shall be minister of music if he is an ordained ministerial member of an Annual Conference, or director of music if he is a layman.[1]

It is advisable to give youth opportunity to express their preferences when nominations are being made for their teachers.

In the quarterly conference responsibility for nominating the persons who are to be elected to leadership is fixed in the nominating committee. The pastor is chairman of this committee. The importance of the nominating committee can hardly be overstated. Many churches favor making it a permanent committee (though its membership changes) continually at work.

In the commission on education responsibility for nominations should be fixed in the committee on recruiting and training leaders. Even in commissions not following the committee plan otherwise, it is suggested that nomination of teachers and leaders for election by the commission be the responsibility of a committee. This should be a continuing committee with responsibility for training leaders as well as recruiting them. Some church schools include in this committee the church-school superintendent, the three division superintendents, the pastor, and the director or minister of education, or educational assistant if there is one. Other church schools feel that these officers have a full work load without this responsibility. In any event, these officers should have close communication with the committee.

In classes or groups which select teachers and other leaders, responsibility for nominations may well be fixed in a class or group committee chosen democratically.

Too often the responsibility for making nominations to the electing bodies is casually handled. And too often the electing bodies are bypassed entirely. The securing of teachers and other workers is thus left to the pastor or church-school superintendent or division superintendent with little or no assistance from anyone else.

Part of the answer to the question "How do you get teachers?" is in the care with which a procedure is thought through and followed. In connection with this procedure there should be an understanding as to where responsibility rests, as has been illustrated in the foregoing section.

Having a Plan for Securing and Training Leaders

When the question "How do you get teachers?" is responded to with this question, "Do you have a plan for getting them?" the reply often is, "What do you mean by a plan? No, we just go out and get them— or try to."

Our search is not for *the* plan. There is no such thing. Every church will want to work out its own. But experience, accumulating over many years, shows that certain things work. These should be considered. They include items of policy as well as procedure. The following are elements which merit consideration as a plan is developed to provide an answer to our question, "How do you get teachers?"

Creating Favorable Conditions

The spiritual vitality of the church can often be measured by the ease or difficulty with which its leaders and workers are secured. In a church whose members truly are Christ's disciples, leadership emerges naturally and enthusiastically. A disciple is one who has committed himself so wholeheartedly that he does not resist the idea of serving. Indeed he seeks ways to serve. It follows, then, that permanent solution of the teacher problem rests upon the degree of discipleship which is achieved in the congregation.

Is lifting the level of discipleship in a congregation something that can be done? Fortunately, the answer is yes. Our faith supports us. Our whole Christian endeavor is to that end. But what specific things could a commission on education do to help lift the level?

Specifically, if the church school is producing Christians who are ready and anxious to work, that church school is helping raise the level of discipleship in the congregation. The commission on education can direct the church school to this end. This is discussed at some length in Chapter III. The church school can guide pupils into such commitment to serve Christ and his church that the pupils are disappointed and confused if they do not find ways to work for him.

Thus, the church school should be a "growing edge" of the church. Its chief business is introducing persons to Christ and guiding them in Christian development. In this process, the church school interprets Christianity. Continually the leaders should face this question: "Does the pupil (regardless of age) get the impression that a Christian can be a *spectator*, or does he get the impression that a Christian must be a *participant*, in the struggle to bring Christ's Way to all people?"

Every class or group of adults should be a recruiting station for the leadership the church school needs. It should be considered an honor to leave a class and go into service somewhere in the church school. The teachers or planning committees of adult classes should be encouraged to produce from the membership of their classes a due proportion of persons able and willing to be chosen as church-school leaders. In a church school having limited tenure for teachers there can be a steady flow from the membership of adult classes into the teaching jobs and then back again into the adult classes. This is one meaning of "rotation in office" which is strongly encouraged.

This spirit of service can so characterize a church school that new members coming into classes and groups will find it contagious. Recruiting of new members in church school can be on the basis of "Come help us serve" instead of "Come let us serve you."

It all adds up. In course of time—years perhaps, but surely—it will no longer be difficult to secure teachers and workers. There will be workers for every place of service because an adequate interpretation and practicing of discipleship will have come to characterize the congregation. Too idealistic? Not unless one feels that Christianity is too idealistic.

The first step in a plan for solving the teacher problem is to create favorable conditions, making it normal for persons to be willing to serve the Master by serving in the church school.

Adopting Limited Tenure

Several considerations support the recommendation that the commission on education should seriously consider adopting a policy of limiting the time a person may serve in an office or as a teacher. Yet not all agree that it is wise. Consider the following and make your own decisions.

It is the policy of some denominations that all officers and teachers and workers in the church school shall be elected annually. That is, the term of office for every worker is one year. That far the policy of the denomination can take us.

However, a policy locally adopted to control re-election is often considered wise. Part of the answer to our question, "How do you get teachers?" is to be found in being able to say, "We are asking you to take this job for not longer than this specified period of time." The period will vary according to the policy you adopt.

There is good reasoning back of this idea.

Psychologically, a person is better prepared to accept a responsibility if the time the responsibility is to end is understood in advance. Again and again church-school superintendents have reported, "We have found it easier to secure all the teachers we can use now that we can tell them when they will be through, than it was to maintain a minimum teaching staff when we kept teachers indefinitely." As a general rule a church school can more easily be staffed under a policy of limited tenure than without it. A growing body of experience seems to suggest that some reasonable policy for change in teachers and leaders should be the rule rather than the exception.

Likewise, the idea is in harmony with one of the basic facts of Christianity, namely, that the Christian is one who serves. Every Christian should have opportunity to serve in the church, indeed should be expected to serve. Not all members of the congregation should be asked to serve as teachers, but a far greater proportion should be than are, and all should be asked to serve somewhere.

There are different ways of working out limited tenure in the church school. Putting together ideas from various sources, here is one approach, offered as an illustration:

1. The commission on education gives careful thought to the idea of limited tenure. It does not make a quick decision. Opportunity is given for discussion by teachers, parents, and others. It may require months before a policy is adopted, and even then the policy is subject to change in the light of experience. It is helpful if the teachers themselves request the commission to adopt limited tenure.

2. The policy applies throughout the school and without exceptions unless those exceptions are specifically embodied in the policy. It goes into effect at a date announced in advance.

3. Embodied in the plan is the decision not to ask anyone to start teaching without preparation. Persons are invited to "prepare to teach" rather than "to teach." Then when persons are ready, they move into the teaching responsibility. There is provision, as discussed later, for all incoming teachers to make preparation.

4. The maximum period of service is stated clearly. Here is an illustration:

> Teachers—two consecutive one-year terms, total two years
>
> Department superintendents—two consecutive one-year terms, total two years
>
> Division superintendents—three consecutive one-year terms, total three years
>
> General officers—four consecutive one-year terms, total four years

Naturally the length of the maximum period of service decided upon will vary from church to church depending on what seems best locally. In deciding, consideration should be given to the trend toward team or group teaching. Obviously, shorter tenure is less disruptive where several teachers work together to serve the same class. There can be continuity even with some dropping out and others being added.

5. The periods of service are staggered so as to avoid starting at any given time with all new teachers. This may necessitate bringing in teachers at the midyear period or even on a quarterly schedule.

6. When one's period of service is over he has the option of:

a) Returning to his former status (such as being an active member of a class) with no further teaching obligation, for one year, while carrying no stated responsibility;

25

b) Embracing the opportunity the church provides for reading, study, observation, but subject to call for temporary teaching in an emergency (the training opportunities involved here are discussed later) ;

c) Shifting to some other job if mutually agreeable.

7. One year after the end of the period of service, the person may again come back into service as a teacher or other leader if mutually desired, but not necessarily at the same job as he held before.

Limited tenure works in large and in small churches. The way it is applied will vary, but its usefulness does not depend on size. Even in communities where only a very small number of persons are available to teach, limited tenure has sometimes proved helpful, though one's first impression might be to the contrary.

Having Leadership Standards

Consciously or otherwise, we all have in mind certain qualities that we like to see in teachers. The degree to which such standards are formally agreed upon and followed is a matter for the commission on education to decide. Faced with the fact that a teacher is proving unsatisfactory, it is often possible to think back and to realize that unfavorable qualities were recognizable in the person at the outset. Had reasonable standards been enforced, the person might have found service in another relationship better suited.

It has not proved possible to draw up *the* list of standards applicable everywhere. This is a matter for local determination. But these items come to mind: ability to teach and lead, time available, age, personality, education, Christian character, willingness to prepare, personal habits and standards. Personal commitment to Christ and his Way certainly should head any list.

Our age-group specialists have given us suggestions about workers in three divisions:

A worker with children should: sincerely love children; have good health, vision, and pleasing voice; be able to work with hands; move about calmly; understand each child and why he acts as he does; be alert to small things that affect children; make flexible plans; be patient; wait until the right time to give guidance; anticipate and prevent difficulties.

A worker with youth should: be a mature adult; be attractively Christian; enjoy adventure; be a learner; have energy to play with and cheer for youth; know how to plan and work with youth; be sharply aware of age differences that require different methods and materials; rejoice more in growth in a young person than in programs "put over."

26

A leader of adults should: have a wide range of adult experience; face facts squarely; use his head instead of his habits; live what he teaches; use experience—past and present; teach to bring about changes in peoples' lives.

Knowing Leadership Needs

The idea here is a simple one. If you need a teacher for next Sunday, it is probably too late to do a good job of getting one. But if you need a teacher for next year, you have time to proceed successfully. Make it a point to know in advance what your needs are going to be. Although exactness is not possible, reasonably good estimates can be made of probable future needs for teachers and other workers over a given period of time.

How many new teachers and other workers did you need for replacement last year, or during the past two years? If these were normal years, you have a basis for estimating your future needs.

What additional workers will you need because of expansion which you plan? How many new classes and how many "outpost" classes are to be started during the coming year? Do you need an additional nursery home visitor, an adult home visitor, a youth worker? Each of your three age-group divisions should give thought to this matter.

Do you contemplate any changes in the leadership of existing groups, such as a shift to team teaching or a panel of teachers, at any point in the school? Should any classes be divided? Are you planning substitute teachers and assistant teachers anywhere?

Your record of past needs, together with plans for expansion, will provide the information you need. Long-range, advance knowledge of leadership needs merits a place in any approach to solving the question, "How do we get teachers?"

Choosing Leaders Wisely

The advisability of choosing prospective leaders in accordance with good standards (p. 26) is apparent. Yet too often selections are made thoughtlessly. We know better, but frequently yield to the temptation to make snap judgments.

In the preceding section on "Fixing Responsibility for Providing Leaders" provisions for nominating and electing teachers and officers are outlined. Our problem arises at the point of how we use these provisions. For instance:

Too often the nominating committee of quarterly conference is not called to meet until just after morning church service to listen to and give rubber-stamp approval to a list of nominations which the pastor hurriedly thought up the night before, and the list is submitted to quarterly conference that afternoon. Fortunately this is a gross caricature of what takes place in some churches. But unfortunately it is factual reporting of what takes place in others. This could not be called careful selection of leaders.

The quarterly conference elects important general officers of the church school. Its nominating committee should be a year-round committee. It should meet a number of times during the year. It should visit through the church, know accurately the requirements of every job for which it makes nominations. It should carefully review the membership of the church—the whole list of possibilities, not just a few persons who happen to come to mind. Too often the nominating committee overlooks much fine material. There should be careful fitting of person to job. Of course the list of standards (discussed above) should be considered in each case.

The same applies for persons selected by the commission on education and persons selected by classes and groups.

Cynically, one could observe that our problem is not selecting but rather finding persons who may be selected. We gain the impression that there simply are not enough persons available. Thus the idea of selection would seem to be a luxury. Here our faith and Christian determination should come into action. In the Lord's work what needs to be done can be done. Somewhere there is a solution. The fainthearted give up. But the true Christian worker proceeds diligently and finds a solution. One very rarely encounters a situation where it can accurately be said that no one is available for selection.

A moment's thought indicates that the careful selection of the persons to be invited to take office is a necessity in any plan for solving the leadership problem. Do you have a plan for the wise selection of leaders? Give the plan a chance to work.

Inviting Leaders Intelligently

"Say, you would not be interested in teaching in the junior department, would you?" This could hardly be advocated as a way to invite a person to begin the process of becoming a teacher.

Inviting leaders intelligently does not mean that it will be done in the same way in all churches. Again, we are not searching for *the* way. But it is profitable to give thought to what constitutes good procedure.

Bear in mind the suggestions made earlier about a period of preparation before one assumes responsibility. Many times resistance vanishes when one is invited to prepare for a job, rather than asked to assume the job immediately.

And recall, too, the advantage of being able to tell the prospect when the job will be over. To say when the job begins and when it ends is intelligent procedure.

Here are some specifics:

Service in the church is a normal responsibility of all Christians. It is reasonable that qualified persons take their turn at the jobs needing to be done. When asking one to serve, an attitude of apology is out of place. Be able to say to the person that his selection has been the subject of prayer and that it is the judgment of those handling the matter that he is the person who should assume the responsibility. To fulfill this, it is necessary that the selection be done with intelligence and integrity. If an *already overworked* person refuses to take additional responsibility, that refusal is justified. It may be an indictment of the group doing the selecting.

Do not always press for immediate answers. Allow the person time prayerfully to consider the invitation. As those responsible for inviting have taken time and have prayed, give the person time for prayer. Allow the Holy Spirit to invite also.

The job should be carefully explained. Difficulties that may be involved should not be evaded. But in discussing the job, joy in service of the Master should predominate over difficulties. Inspire the person with the realization of the far-reaching consequences of the service he is to render and how much it means in the work of the church and God's kingdom.

Here is an ideal toward which to strive: Do the selecting so wisely and the inviting so intelligently that a refusal would come as a real shock, unless of course there were reasons for refusal that the committee could not have known. Indeed, it is shocking to think that a Christian, unless for valid reason, would refuse a Christian responsibility. Before extending an invitation, be as sure as is humanly possible that it is the responsibility of the individual to accept. Remember it is normal for a *Christian* to accept if he understands that it is his responsibility.

Training Leaders Thoroughly

The trained worker not only serves more worthily, but contributes to the securing of other workers. People more readily associate themselves with a group of workers who are growing and getting things done. Training leads to success. The trained teacher is more apt to be happy in his work than the untrained one.

But in the average church school how can a program of training be carried on?

Church schools which provide a period of training before persons assume responsibility as teachers, frequently conduct training classes during sessions of the church school. These can be at the Sunday-school hour, during the Sunday evening fellowship, or at some other time when the church school is in session. Thus they avoid setting up an additional schedule. A simple arrangement, well within the ability of even the smallest school, is to offer at the Sunday-school hour one training course a year which lasts for six or more consecutive Sundays. From this very modest approach the plan can expand until there is a continuing program of training offering several courses at a time. A plan within the reach of most church schools is to offer a course each quarter for a given number of Sundays—four times a year. Variations are endless. Tailor the plan to fit your need.

The leadership committee in the commission on education should plan well in advance the courses that will be offered. It is not unrealistic for the schedule of courses to be set up two or three years in advance. This makes it possible to provide the wide range of different kinds of courses needed in various age groups. Whether these will be credit training courses or not depends on your resources. The catalog of training courses from your general board of education will suggest titles and texts. These can be used in informal courses as well as in credit courses.

Where does a church school secure leaders for such a training program? The answer is: find them locally, import them, or produce them yourself. Often competent leaders for training courses live in the community and can be secured if invited sufficiently in advance. Often good training work can be done by inexperienced leaders if they are given sufficient time to prepare and are given proper materials for reading and study.

Beyond the local church, within almost every district, there are every year Christian workers' schools, laboratory schools, and other training opportunities. Participation in these can and should be made a part of the obligations assumed by persons who agree to teach. The policy of discussing this obligation with every new teacher should accompany the plan of offering training courses within the local church and participating in other training opportunities. We have been far too modest in what we require of the persons who teach in our church schools.

Where team teaching is used, it is easy to arrange periods when some of the teachers can be released to take these training courses. The same is true with substitute teachers.

There are likewise many informal opportunities to increase one's skills as a teacher. Guided reading is high on the list of such. The leadership committee of the commission on education has the continuing responsibility of guiding the teaching staff in helpful reading. This calls for ingenuity and application, but success here is rewarding.

The several workers' conference meetings each year (for workers and prospective workers) offer splendid opportunity to help in the training of teachers. Lectures by educational leaders in the community, discussion panels, problem-solving sessions, book reviews, filmstrips with discussion, the simple talking over of the work—all these contribute to the training of teachers. Team teaching, panels of teachers, and the plan of having substitute teachers offer continuing opportunity for training. The less skilled associated with the more skilled gives a natural setting for in-service training to take place. An uninformed, but intelligent and willing person, associated with experienced teachers in a teaching team can rapidly acquire skill. Observing skilled teachers at work yields good dividends.

Fortunate is the teacher who works in a school where there is good supervision. Supervision, thought of as wise helpfulness, speeds the acquisition of skills on the part of teachers. This is discussed further on p. 94.

Not the least of the informal training opportunities available to all schools, small and large, are periodic times of evaluation and discussion of the work. In workers' conference, or any grouping of teachers and leaders, a serious and creative discussion, based on careful analysis of what is going on, can lead to increased effectiveness on the part of the leadership.

The recommendation to train leaders thoroughly, and keep on training them in service, merits the serious consideration of every church school facing the question, "How do we get teachers?"

Developing Leaders Continually

In these days of mobile population, if a church school loses a good leader because he moves away, the compensating thought is that some other church school can profit by his skill. Yet the only leaders many church schools have are the leaders they produce. So we give serious thought to the idea of developing a leadership within the church school, as a continuing project.

Children and youth can be guided in such a way that they mature

31

into excellent Christian leaders. The development of leadership qualities among adults is common procedure. As we realize that everyone exerts some leadership, we recognize that Christian training in general is in a sense leadership development. Actually, this is the foundation of all leadership development. But specialized attention can be given to developing leaders. Discover and interest promising young people in taking responsibility in their own groups. Long before he is old enough to be a teacher, special attention can be given to the Christian growth of a promising young person. A word of encouragement and the assignment of responsibility in keeping with growing ability aid in developing workers. Above all, the development in young people of a sense of mission and a realization of their privilege to serve Christ leads to service in the work of the church.

But the development of leaders is by no means limited to young persons. Adult leaders can be grown likewise. Maintain a long-range list of prospective teachers and keep cultivating it. Months and even years of shaping attitudes and kindling ideals of service build up a reserve from which leaders may be drawn.

Read again the statement on p. 23 about every adult class producing leaders for the church school. Here is a resource of great significance.

The idea of growing your own leaders is well worth including in the plan you are developing to solve the leadership problem in your church school.

Correcting Leadership Misfits

The number of ineffective leaders—misfits—will be small if wise procedures have been followed in the selection of leaders. But when misfits are recognized, one or another of the following can be done:

Let time take care of the matter. Sometimes this would be procrastination and evasion of responsibility. But sometimes if the misfit is not doing great harm, it would be the wisest course—particularly if in your church school you have limited tenure.

Let rotation in office and limited tenure (see p. 24) take care of the matter. Unless the situation is quite serious, a misfit in a particular office or other responsibility can be endured until the person's period of service is terminated under your limited tenure plan.

There is always the radical possibility of dismissing the individual and depriving him of his place of service. That often is unchristian, however, and usually creates more problems than it solves. It is to be remembered that the misfit is a person and as such is the subject of the Christian concern of his fellow workers. There should be clear justification for any such drastic procedure as dismissing a Christian worker.

Often an individual who is not serving effectively in one relationship can be shifted to another with real satisfaction to all concerned. This is a common and highly successful procedure.

Sometimes the misfit can be induced to resign his place of specialized leadership. This is a possibility to be included in this list, but does not happen often.

Ideally, the finest procedure is to redeem the misfit right there in his own job. This takes time, understanding, and consecration to the task, but it is often possible and always is worthwhile.

It is usually best that decisions in this matter be made by the commission on education rather than for an administrator, as an individual, to do it. Each case is more or less unique and requires special handling. There are few, if any, set rules. Prayerful thought and discreet consultation will generally care for these problems.

Supporting Leaders Wholeheartedly

A vital part of maintaining an adequate teaching force is good morale. Friendliness, cordiality, enthusiasm, and consecration belong in this picture.

A telephone call to a teacher, expressing appreciation for good work done, often works wonders in promoting an increased devotion to the task. Occasional commendation from the pulpit referring to the entire teaching group is most helpful. Appreciation dinners and other occasions honoring workers are highly successful. Visiting workers in their homes for the primary purpose of revealing appreciation is very fruitful. Many churches use installation and consecration services in which not only the teachers and leaders, but also the congregation are involved.

To proceed intelligently in securing and training leaders and getting them to work, and then failing to support them wholeheartedly, is not reasonable. The whole matter rounds out joyously when we undergird, with true respect and appreciation, these fine teachers and leaders who serve so selflessly.

This chapter began by facing the question, "How do you get teachers?" A general outline for an answer was given: Understand what leadership is, fix responsibility for providing leadership, and have a plan. Elements that might be considered in the development of such a plan have been discussed. A request to your denominational board of education will bring you specific helps in terms of your own denomination. What steps do you plan to take in providing your own answer to the question, "How do you get teachers?"

3

COMMITMENT TO CHRIST AND THE CHURCH

The church exists to lead persons to commit themselves to God through Christ and to join and participate in its holy fellowship and work. In no way can the church better do this than through its church school! But this does not happen automatically.

By its very nature the church school is in the business of evangelism. Education that is not evangelistic is not Christian. One works in vain who teaches *about* Christ without introducing his pupils *to* Christ. We repudiate the mistaken idea that the teacher carries a pupil only so far, and then someone called an evangelist must take over and lead the pupil the rest of the way. The teacher must not neglect this part of the job, else he is not a Christian teacher.

The church school has an organization and a corps of teachers and workers needing only to be inspired and guided into being an effective evangelistic force. In this chapter we will consider ways in which the church school can guide persons to commit themselves to Christ and to unite with his church.

Responsibility for planning evangelism in the church school resides in the commission on education, which has a committee or a person to lead in its consideration (see also p. 152). Responsibility for administering these plans resides in the church-school superintendent and the other officers. Responsibility for carrying them out resides in the teachers and in various other persons and groups as may be determined and in every Christian connected in any way with the enterprise.

What Is Evangelism in the Church School?

In our Christian vocabulary there are many wonderful words—stewardship, missions, evangelism, redemption, salvation, and others. Each contributes to a description of the work of the church, though from a different angle. They interrelate and overlap. Where one ends and the other begins is difficult to say.

We single out one of these words. Within the processes of Christian education exactly what is meant by evangelism? Or, more simply, what is evangelism in the church school?

The answer used in this book is this: By evangelism in the church school we mean two related matters—guiding persons to commit themselves (1) to Christian discipleship through complete love for and surrender to Christ as Lord and Savior, and (2) to assuming the vows of church membership and participating in the work and fellowship of the church.

Though these two matters are related, they are two distinct experiences involving separate commitments. It is important that this be understood.

The position is taken that within the experiences of Christian education there can be such a thing as deep, life-conditioning commitment. Further, the position is taken that unless there is that commitment, Christian education has failed. For further consideration of the meaning of commitment see also p. 37.

The Pastor's Role in Church School Evangelism

The pastor is the pastor of his whole church—of all the people and of all the organizations in the church. He prays for and wisely guides every group. They are all parts of his church, and all are his vital concern. In evangelism he thinks of every person and every group as helping, as all work together.

Because of its vast potential, he thinks of the church school as a chief agency for evangelism. He thinks of teachers as evangelists, as extensions of his own heart and his own arms. He counsels with them, encourages them, and looks on them as fellow workers.

What is the pastor's role in church-school evangelism? In *kind* it is the same as in all other phases of the life of his church. To all of them he is pastor and leader, and from all of them he expects evangelistic results. But in *degree* he looks to the church school for larger evangelistic results because it has larger opportunity. And in expecting this, he functions continually as encourager, as counselor, and as guide. The pastor is the church school's head coach in evangelism.

The Role of the Commission on Education and the Commission on Membership and Evangelism

The commission on education is responsible for the church school. To avoid confusion in administration and program this must be recognized. Evangelism (in this context) can be accomplished by the Holy Spirit through Christian education. Therefore, the commission on education is responsible for evangelism in the church school. *But not by itself alone.* The commission on membership and evangelism has an important supporting role, effective in at least three ways:

1. Through the assistance the commission on membership and evangelism can give the commission on education in planning the evangelistic program of the church school, by meeting with the commission on education one or more times each year in a planning session. This is discussed later in this chapter.

2. Through cross representation in membership between the two commissions (see p. 153). Specifically, it is suggested that the representative of the commission on membership and evangelism to the commission on education be selected as chairman of the committee on winning pupils to Christ and church membership of the commission on education.

3. Through frequent consultation between the two commission chairmen, not only in the official board as total program is discussed but informally to utilize resources of the commission on membership and evangelism to aid in the evangelistic work of the church school as may be desirable.

Unfortunately the two commissions sometimes devise a working relationship whereby the commission on education lists all prospective church members who are in the church school and then turns those prospects over to the commission on membership and evangelism to be won to Christ and church membership. This plan has a glaring fault. If carried to an extreme, it relieves the teacher of evangelistic responsibility. That takes the heart out of Christian education. While there should never be a spirit of exclusiveness in connection with any list of persons who may be won to Christ and the church, and while all help from all quarters should be welcomed, co-operation should be carried on in such a way as not to undermine the true work of a Christian teacher. It is the teacher's responsibility to win pupils to Christ and the church.

Elements in the Personal Evangelistic Ability of Teachers

An Understanding of WHY Evangelism Is the Teacher's Task

It is the intent of the Christian gospel that those who receive its teaching shall follow its Christ. The gospel is not just a body of content to be learned or just a matter for contemplation. Its basic nature calls for deep, life-changing commitment to Christ. It is a matter for action, following its Divine Leader. It is unnatural and tragically superficial to try to teach *about* Christ and not introduce persons *to* Christ.

Together with preaching and witnessing, teaching is enjoined by Christ as a way to bring people to him. The Christian teacher stands in the glorious company of those who, through all Christian centuries, have led men and women and children to the Master. Teaching that does not lead to Christ cannot be called Christian teaching.

With acceptance of the fact that the lay people of the church must work as evangelists along with the pastor, the Christian teacher naturally takes his place among those who work to lead others to Christ and the church.

An Understanding of WHAT Commitment to Christ and to the Church Means

What does commitment to Christ mean?

But first, what is commitment?

In the marriage ceremony we see an example. In marriage at its best sincere Christians truly in love and ready for total sacrifice to each other should occasion demand, pledge themselves each to the other in every respect without reservation. Instead of compromising personality and individual dignity, it enhances them. This is commitment.

In the baptism of infants parents solemnly assume responsibility for guiding the young life in the Christian Way. It is a clear-cut and absolute assumption of an obligation from which there can with integrity be no turning back. This is commitment.

Commitment to Christ gathers up all that is finest in commitment on the human level and goes on to an even higher conception. An older generation used the term "surrender." Have we found a better term? They (and Paul) talked of enslavement. Have we thought of a clearer description? Yet the term we use is immaterial. It may change as word meanings change. But the reality we seek to describe does not change. If there is such a thing as absolute (and I believe there is), here is one. In the finest expression of Christianity, the Christian is one who has put Christ in absolute control of his life. In carrying out this relationship the Christian may stumble and blunder and because of his finiteness fail to reach his high goal in many, many respects. But that does not compromise the fact of his commitment.

And those thus committed know the blessed corollary. Through such enslavement they achieve true freedom.

From older childhood through adulthood commitment to Christ means the surrender to God's purposes of all that one has and is without reservation. It is a deeply personal matter. It takes place within one's inmost self, sometimes suddenly but more often gradually—so gradually that one can find himself completely committed without realizing when it happened. He simply realizes that he has "always" been committed. And there is recommitment many, many times as one increasingly understands.

Growing up in the faith is highly desirable. Yet it involves some hazards. Commitment can be so matter-of-course that when testing times come it turns out to be superficial. It is wholesome for Christians continually to strengthen the bonds between themselves and Christ.

It is important that the deep significance of commitment be understood by the teacher. Two aspects especially command attention: (a) it is only through positive commitment that a life can anchor itself in God in all the wonder and richness that entails; (b) it is not adequate to think of commitment as one identifiable event. New insights into God's will occasion new affirmations of commitment. Thus commitment is a growing thing.

Happily commitment has meaning on all levels of maturity, differing of course in degree of comprehension, but real for all ages mature enough to comprehend. This is discussed later.

What does commitment to the church mean?

38

Naturally it means assuming the vows of church membership. But it means more than that. Commitment to the church means wholehearted participation in the fellowship of the believers for the worship of God, for service to his children everywhere, for the guidance and encouragement of others, and for the development and strengthening of one's own Christian living. All this is based on the conviction that the church is God's agency for the salvation of mankind. Denominational loyalty and local church loyalty are deeply involved, if participation is to be genuine. In short a Christian must be a disciple, and a disciple exercises his discipleship through the church as well as in other ways. Since a Christian is a *participant* in the work and not just a *spectator*, it inescapably follows that he is committed to the working church.

An Understanding of HOW a Teacher Functions as an Evangelist

How can a teacher be an evangelist?

One finds the answer to this question in the heart more than in accuracy of procedures. Evangelism is more a way of life than a set of rules. A teacher who has the heart of an evangelist will be one regardless of his understanding of all that is involved.

But there are many guiding lights that can be lit along the way. The six that follow merit consideration. Where team teaching is in effect, most of the following suggestions apply to all members of the teaching team. Specific assignments of responsibility can be made as needed.

1. The *example* one sets, revealing the genuineness of his own commitment, draws others into the Christian Way. For the teacher who would win persons to Christ and the church, this is a sure guide. It is also a sobering thought. We do teach by example.

2. Just as the good shepherd knows his sheep, so the good teacher knows his pupils. Early in this book we noted that our concern is for persons. True evangelism centers in honest concern for persons. It is suggested that every teacher of persons old enough to make the serious commitments involved, maintain a *Responsibility List for Evangelism.* Here the teacher writes the names of those in his group who are not members of the church. Some of these may be committed Christians who have not yet assumed church membership. Some may not be. In any case, each one on the list is a *responsibility* of the teacher. As persons on the list unite with the church, their names are removed. As new persons not members of the church join the group, their names are added. A *Responsibility List* should be as normal a part of the working tools of a teacher as literature, the hymnal, and the Bible.

3. *Intercessory prayer* is an inevitable practice of the teacher who is

concerned for the spiritual development of persons entrusted to him. Indeed, intercessory prayer is central in our evangelistic endeavors. The teacher who is also a shepherd will pray earnestly for his pupils, for each one by name. The *Responsibility List* thus becomes a *prayer list*. This fact is a guiding light that is brightly lit, pointing the way of evangelism in the church school.

4. It is possible to *teach for Christian commitment*. A teacher earnestly wanting to encourage commitments will think through what this means and how it can be done. Consider these suggestions:

a) The teacher's mind will be focused on this great goal of his teaching. That is, the teacher is himself conditioned in the desired direction. In preparing and conducting the class session this is always in the background of his thinking.

b) The teacher will be alert to discover and use the opportunities which arise in the lessons to encourage Christian commitment.

c) The portrayal of Christ, as the subject arises from time to time, invariably will be warmhearted and appealing. Christ's claim on our lives will emerge naturally and positively.

d) Though mindful of its faults, the teacher will reveal his own loyalty to and love for the church. He will seek to aid pupils in having a like attitude, by his example and unstudied influence as well as by direct purposing, as there is occasion.

But in all this there must be balance and reasonableness. Fanaticism, pressure, boring repetition will defeat rather than aid in teaching for Christian commitment.

5. The teacher serves as an evangelist through personal conversations with his pupils. Who is better fitted to lead a person to Christian commitment than a concerned teacher who maintains close, friendly, inspiring contact with his pupils? And what occasion could be more appropriate than a quiet personal conversation?

6. Any listing of how a teacher functions as an evangelist must include the teacher's co-operation in the larger evangelistic activities of the church as a whole. The evangelistic teacher knows about and, as is appropriate, helps with the evangelistic plans of the pastor and the commission on membership and evangelism as well as the commission on education.

An Understanding of Evangelism for Various Ages

It is imperative that those who guide a church school clearly understand evangelism with children, with youth, and with adults. Only brief comments can be made here, but the membership manuals of the church and the evangelistic literature of the general board of education for use in the church school, especially the basic age-group manuals, should be studied.

Children are "members of the kingdom of God" and are a part of the church family. This determines our approach to evangelism with children. When they are old enough to understand and to make up their own minds, they are to be encouraged to make for themselves definite commitment to Christ and the church. Children thus committing themselves are not thought of as blackhearted sinners accepting salvation. Yet even children can defy God and say "no" to him. They, too, must accept his help in restoring relationship to their Heavenly Father through Christ, and understandingly committing themselves to him.

Ability to understand what is involved in church membership and the requisite commitment to God through Christ will come to children at different ages. Thus it is unwise to establish a fixed age to encourage church membership. But there is widespread approval for the position that it often is premature to think of this step before the age of older juniors, which usually is eleven. Some may be ready before, but very few. Indeed there are those who feel the junior-high age is young enough.

Throughout their lives there will be occasions of recommitment and deeper commitment as their experience and understanding grow. From birth until this time of personal commitment the church school surrounds them with expressions of God's love, teaches them the Christian religion as they are progressively able to understand, and establishes them in the Christian life.

Our approach to evangelism with youth is between that of children and adults, having some of the nature of both because such characterizes youth. As youth matures, evidences of alignment with evil occur in some persons. The point of view that is normal concerning children, that they are "within the Kingdom," may become unrealistic. In such cases repudiation of evil must accompany commitment to good. The basic requirements of "repentance, faith, and obedience" apply. Salvation from something to something must actually take place. In the case of other youth, particularly younger youth, the situation often is very similar to that of older children.

The adult who has not assumed the vows of church membership *may* be a believing Christian who has not particularly resisted uniting with the church but who has, for one reason or another, been overlooked in the evangelistic activities of the church. This individual may be a committed Christian needing only to be guided into church membership.

But usually this is not the case. The adult who is not a church member usually is not a truly committed Christian and needs full encouragement and help in reaching Christian commitment and church membership.

Ability to Handle Related Problems

In the consideration of elements in the personal evangelistic ability of teachers, it is helpful to include ability to handle wisely problems in evangelism related to theology, Christian doctrine, the Bible, modern living, and the like.

A teacher without a reasonable understanding of theology will have difficulty in helping an unbeliever who does know something of theology. And such a teacher is in danger of misleading persons who know nothing of theology. The same is true in related matters, mentioned above.

This leads to the conclusion that provision must be made to help teachers acquire a reasonable amount of background in these matters.

A Personal Life of Deep Spirituality

Quite understandably the evangelistic ability of a teacher can hardly be greater than the spiritual quality of his life. Those who guide a church school have the opportunity and the responsibility of encouraging all teachers and leaders in this matter. It is easy to list factors that are involved: prayer habits, Bible reading, church attendance and participation, private worship, Christian service, stewardship, and the like. One can be guided by such a list as he progresses toward deeper spirituality in personal living. But there is more to it. Sincerely wanting to live closer to Christ and his way must govern in a life if the activities commonly associated with Christian development are to lead to the splendor of truly spiritual personality.

Elements in a Program of Evangelism
in the Church School

What is meant by "a program of evangelism" in the church school? How does one get hold of it?

As is true so often in the work of the church, the answer must be worked out locally. Programs developed afar off seldom fit exactly. There can be no escaping the necessity for each local church school patiently and prayerfully putting together its own plan for evangelism. But in the process it can avail itself of ideas that have proved helpful in other church schools and that emerge out of experience. The following are elements worthy of consideration.

Maintenance of Educational Procedures

Christian education is not accurately understood as a cold, logical process of the mind. It gives welcome place to the emotions as well as the mind. It undertakes to embrace all that is authentic in whatever helps lives, through teaching, change toward Christ. Its focus is on persons.

Thus it does not include high pressures that induce superficial commitments. It grades its efforts in terms of the maturity of persons and does not elicit adult reactions from children and younger youth.

In warmly encouraging commitments to Christ and to church membership, the church school remains "in character" as the church teaching. We have heeded the plea of John Wesley, "Let us unite the two so long divided, knowledge and vital piety." In our evangelism we use procedures in accord with good Christian education.

Orientation of New Teachers and Leaders

Consider the splendid things which might result if it were an invariable rule to have a serious conversation with every new teacher and worker to talk over opportunities and responsibilities. Who could measure the gains a church school could make evangelistically if every new teacher, right at the beginning of his teaching career, were helped to see that he, personally, could lead immortal souls to Christ and to membership in his church!

A review of this chapter will suggest matters appropriate for such a conversation, not overlooking how a teacher functions as an evangelist (see p. 39).

Why not do it?

Actually, it can be done. In some situations the pastor might do it. On circuits and in large churches other leaders could carry this responsibility. Such a conversation with each new teacher could have definite bearing on evangelistic success.

Will this be included in the plans for evangelism in your church school?

Using Opportunities in the Curriculum

Lesson materials are written to help lead persons to Christ and the church. This is true with the materials for all age groups. For the age range at the close of childhood and the beginning of youth they especially encourage life commitment to the Christian Way. They are an immediate aid to the teacher in evangelism. For all ages they undertake continually to encourage the acceptance by the individual of Christian belief, Christian conduct, and Christian commitment.

The alert teacher will note this quality in the lesson materials and will use the opportunities it brings to achieve evangelistic results normal to the age and circumstances of the group he leads.

Encouragement from the Workers' Conference

It is expected that several times a year all teachers and workers in the church school will come together for a full evening (or Sunday afternoon) as the workers' conference. These meetings are discussed on p. 99. Here we focus on their evangelistic possibilities.

One of these meetings, or parts of several, can be used to face three questions treated earlier in this chapter: (a) *Why* is evangelism the task of the teacher? (b) *What* does commitment to Christ and the church mean? (c) *How* can a teacher be an evangelist?

These three tremendously important subjects cannot be covered fully in one meeting, but enough can be done to inform and inspire. Literature can be distributed and discussed. The pastor can open his heart and let the teachers and workers realize afresh the sacredness of their work and the necessity of their doing it well.

Ordering and Using Literature

Booklets and leaflets are available from your general board of education to help teachers and administrators succeed in the evangelistic work of the church school. But despite the excellence of your church's plan for distributing guidance literature, many workers in many local churches never see it.

As you perfect your plans for evangelism, consider making definite provision for the following:

1. Placing orders for evangelistic literature, graded for use by teachers in all three divisions. Have times designated on the calendar for doing this. Fix in some person responsibility for ordering.

2. Distributing the literature wisely. This will include putting it in the hands of new teachers when they are being oriented personally in evangelism as discussed on p. 43 and distributed at workers' conference and in other meetings on evangelism in the church school.

3. Helping leaders to understand and follow the guidance the literature affords. This will require superintendents to master the contents and to plan occasions when it can be discussed.

The Pastor's Class

Among the elements in a program of evangelism in the church school perhaps none holds more significance than the pastor's class. It is important that its purpose be understood and that it be supported and conducted in the effective manner intended. Using the manuals of the church for this purpose, the pastor reviews the progress made in church-school classes and groups in which pupils have been guided toward personal Christian commitments. This presupposes, of course, that the pastor is familiar with the curriculum and how it guides toward church membership. With individual attention to the needs of each pupil, after careful checking, he interprets and encourages decisions just as do the teachers. As pastor he represents the church in the minds of the pupils and aids the transition into the larger fellowship of actual church membership. The pastor's class focuses on older children and younger youth. The idea of a pastor's class, however, has great value for all ages, including adults. Apart from the church school alert pastors continually provide church membership classes for adults uniting with the church.

The Annual School of Evangelistic Teaching

"Do you have a practical plan for training teachers to be evangelists?"

This question should be asked officially in connection with reports at quarterly conference.

This question is what a large part of this chapter is about. An intelligent response to the need which it implies is the most important business a church school could be up to. As part of a plan calculated to make a vigorous affirmative answer possible, we propose *an annual school of evangelistic teaching*.

This idea is beyond the trial stage in some sections and has settled down into an established routine. But it is untried in others. Here, in brief summary, is what it is:

Participants. All teachers and leaders, *including those who work with young children.* They, too, are involved in evangelism, as discussed on p. 40.

Schedule. Minimum of six hours if possible, such as Sunday afternoon plus Monday and Tuesday evenings. Settle for less if absolutely necessary. Yearly repeats prove helpful.

Purpose. To gather together the things said in this chapter, involving some repeats on things undertaken at other times. There are persons not present at the other times, and some things are so important they need to be said more than once to register fully. But basically the purpose is to undertake to do a good total job of getting the church school in the business of evangelism effectively and permanently.

Groupings. Part of the time all meet together. Part of the time meet by division age groups with a fourth group for general officers.

Content. A thorough presentation of the *Why?* *What?* and *How?* already discussed in this chapter, with sufficient time spent on *How?* This can lead to a searching reappraisal of what teaching is, how it is done, and what it is for. It can move some teachers out of the ranks of theorists and make them effective practitioners. It should result in a clearer understanding of the meaning of sin and salvation. One certainly cannot go through a good school of evangelistic teaching and be unmindful of the implications of Christ's command to teach.

A Calendar

A necessary element in a program of evangelism in a church school would be a calendar indicating when, during the year, various things would be done. A class of teachers and pastors wrote this on the chalkboard as a minimum calendar:

—date for the meeting of the commission on education, to which the commission on membership and evangelism is invited, to plan the year's program of evangelism in the church school.

—date for the pastor's class synchronized with junior and junior-high department lesson materials leading to church membership. Additional dates for older youth and adults recommended.

—dates for special evangelistic seasons in church school (illustration: pre-Easter through Mother's Day).

—dates for evangelistic occasions in the whole church and beyond-the-local-church in which the church school can co-operate.

—date for ordering the free evangelistic literature from the general board of education.

—date for the annual school of evangelistic teaching.

—date for the workers' conference meeting to be devoted to evangelism in the church school.

—date for annual check-up on use of *Teacher's Responsibility List for Evangelism.*

Perpetual Review of Statistical Situation

Two things are to be noted here:

1. Month after month is there a steady flow of new members being brought into the church school? To reach anything like its full evangelistic potential a church school must be growing in membership and

attendance, by reaching out into the community for the unchurched.

2. Month after month are members of the church school uniting with the church on profession of faith?

These statistics should be watched closely. They are an index to progress.

Combined Commission Meetings

Once a year, preferably at the beginning of your church school year, devote one full meeting of the commission on education to planning the year's program of evangelism in the church school.

To this meeting invite the full membership of the commission on membership and evangelism. This, of course, is time consuming. Why should it be done?

—to give the commission on membership and evangelism opportunity to contribute, on the planning level, to the program of evangelism in the church school.
—to keep the commission on education in step with the total plans of evangelism in the church as a whole and to insure the informed co-operation of the church school.

The commission on membership and evangelism is present to advise and assist in developing plans. To avoid confusion in administration, the plans are carried out through the commission on education. The two chairmen and the pastor should take the lead in arranging dates for the meeting. Agenda items can be gleaned from this chapter as thought wise.

A Clear Charting of Action

Examine the root of a growing plant. It will be found to have a "growing point." In this chapter as we have discussed winning pupils to Christ and the church, we really have been considering the church school as a "growing point" of the church.

Focus on this idea a moment.

That the church must continually work to reach more and more persons with the Christian message, guide them to commit themselves to God through Christ and come into the fellowship of the church, is well understood. That is a major characteristic of an evangelical church. But how can that best be done? Or, at least, what ways are open to a church for getting it done? Or, what is one way?

There is a simple and workable answer: Through its church school.

In a number of the fastest growing of the giant denominations in America, this idea of the church school serving as the "growing point" for the church has governed for a long time. That is one of the reasons why they are growing so fast. So here we are not dealing with an untried theory. We have here something that works.

Below, a formula will be proposed for your consideration, but first note the simple basic ideas on which the formula rests. There are two of them: (a) It is easier to get unchurched persons to join a class in church school than it is to get them to join the church. That is, the church school provides a relatively easy first contact. (b) Church-school members are more easily won to Christ and church membership than are persons not in church school. The statistics of denomination after denomination support this.

And note: These two basic ideas are not substitutes for other evangelistic procedures regularly and successfully used in local churches. They are in addition to them. They can be a "plus element" or they can be the chief "growing point" for the local church.

There are four steps in the formula which any church school anywhere can follow as it undertakes to serve as a "growing point" for its church:

1. *Get unchurched people into church school.* This must be thought of as a major undertaking, carried on continuously and on as large a scale as possible. It includes persons of all ages—from birth to old age. (The little ones are not yet ready for the vows of church membership, but they will be some day.) It includes not only a steady increase in church-school *membership* but also in *attendance* (see Chap. IV).

2. *Win pupils to Christ.* Through the procedures discussed in this chapter make it a central concern of the entire teaching and leadership personnel to make Christ real in the life of every pupil, young and old, and earnestly encourage those who are mature enough to commit themselves to him.

3. *Guide committed pupils into church membership.* This naturally follows commitment to Christ, but it must not be taken for granted. Church schools undertaking to be a "growing point" for the church major in those procedures which insure that not one member of the church school who is old enough and who truly is a committed Christian is overlooked in the warmhearted, sincere effort to bring persons into church membership.

4. *Conserve church membership.* Bringing persons into church membership is not enough. To insure their continuing as active Christians and as church members, involve them in the responsibilities and the

48

work of the church school and the church, as their maturity and abilities make appropriate. There is a place of service for every disciple. Every disciple should be aided and encouraged to find that place and to serve in it. And as a part of all this the continuing growth of the individual in Christian understanding and service must be insured through participation in church school and church.

These four simple steps are well within the ability of every church school. In its church school every church can have a "growing point."

4

INCREASING CHURCH-SCHOOL MEMBERSHIP AND ATTENDANCE

Why Increase?

Seldom does a Christian mean it literally when he says, "I am not interested in getting people to join the church school or the church. I am interested in getting them to become Christians."

But instances of people being herded into the church without adequate preparation and sometimes without real conviction and commitment have caused justifiable concern and unfortunate reactions. Actually, what Christians really want is for all persons everywhere to become Christians *and* to assume the vows of the church. The place of the church in God's plan of salvation for individuals and for society, when rightly understood, is so exalted and so fundamental that, unhesitatingly, we align ourselves with those working to bring committed persons into the membership of the church.

That brings us to face our attitude toward increasing membership and attendance in the church school.

It is good to bring persons into contact with the church through any of the ways in which the church expresses itself. So it is good to bring persons into contact with the church through the church school. But there are other reasons for increasing church-school membership and attendance. We suggest three. One relates to deep, personal religion; one to the well-being of people in general; and one to the church.

Why increase church-school membership and attendance?

1. *Because* for individual persons, kinship with Christ and a knowledge of the Christian Way mean the difference spiritually between life and death. Christ commanded that his way be taught. The church has created the church school to help carry out this Christian command. The church school, even at its inefficient worst, is still the church engaged in teaching. And that which it exists to teach is so utterly indispensable to persons of all ages that we are zealous to bring every man, woman, and child into its membership and under its influence. The searching, imperative urgency of the gospel for individual lives is clear. How can we be indifferent? The people, as individual souls, *must* have Christian teaching.

2. *Because* man's ancient dependence upon the gospel for life here and hereafter has taken on a new social urgency. If man does not acquire a sense of Christian responsibility to control man's swiftly expanding physical powers in the modern world, including his new powers to destroy himself, we face problems unprecedented in man's history. Indeed, we face those problems in acute form today. But only one American in four has any connection whatever with a church school.

3. *Because* of the supreme importance of the church school to the church of which it is a part.

a) The church wins more persons to Christ through its church school than any other way.

b) The church school produces the bulk of the church's leadership. It develops those inner attitudes of responsibility and Christian obligation upon which church work depends.

c) Aside from its work with adults, the church school is the agency through which the church holds and nurtures children and younger youth who are not yet ready for mature church participation. Without the church school the church would be powerless to do this in modern society. The church as we know it could not survive if it depended solely upon adult recruiting.

d) For persons of all ages the church ministers through preaching, teaching, and witnessing. Adults, youth, and children receive the ministry of Christian teaching primarily through the church school. How important it is that every church school include provision for teaching adults as well as youth and children!

e) There is no other plan in operation or in prospect which gives any reasonable promise of being able to take the place of the church school as the teaching phase of the church.

Thus we commit ourselves to increasing church-school membership and attendance for the sake of every man, woman, and child we can reach. In this chapter we consider ways to do this.

What Do We Seek to Increase?

1. If we look beyond the church school as an institution with its programs and procedures, it is not difficult to realize that what we are undertaking to increase is the participation of individual persons in learning and practicing Christianity. It is well that this be kept in mind. The subtle temptation is always with us to increase the church school for its own sake, or for the sake of bigness. But if our real purpose is clearly and constantly before us, we can enter into the necessary mechanics of increase without hesitation.

2. It is well, likewise, to comprehend the scope of the enterprise for which we seek more members and better attendance. At various places in this book the scope of the "church-school idea" is discussed. Suffice it to say here that the membership increase which we seek is in terms of all of the parts which make up the church school. The Sunday school, the Sunday evening fellowship, the weekday activities, and the home and extension service afford opportunity for the participation of individual persons in learning and practicing Christianity. And all should reach and serve as many persons as possible. Reaching an additional infant through the nursery home roll is church-school membership increase. Adding another to the roll of a Sunday-school class is church-school membership increase. Securing more members for a Tuesday evening *Bible* study group is church-school membership increase. Despite the demands of modern living for new approaches to serving the spiritual needs of the people, many of us have been slow to realize that the church is in the business of Christian education wherever and whenever people can be reached and served. Increasing church-school membership today is a much more comprehensive thing than was getting more members in Sunday school in a former day.

Who are these persons whom we are seeking? It has been said, above, that reaching an additional infant through the nursery home roll is church-school membership increase. But is the full significance of this understood? Do the membership cultivation superintendent (discussed in the following pages) and those associated with him in their work of securing more members in the church school fully comprehend how extensive this project is which we call the church school?

Literally, every person from birth to death is our concern. We are thinking about:

Children. Too often the church school thinks of prospective members only in terms of persons mature enough to be consulted in the matter of enrolling and attending. And thereby we miss many. Observe:

—The new-born baby is a prospect for our nursery home roll. Interest and concern adequately expressed may assure his being in the nursery class when he is old enough to come. And frequently parents are brought into the church school because of this concern expressed for their baby.

—The two- and three-year-olds, who as yet "cannot discern between their right hand and their left," are in the focus of our concern for our nursery groups.

—The children not yet in public school, but whose minds are open to the Master are prospects.

—The sturdy boys and girls now in public school, and rapidly developing their attitudes and life habits, are prospects.

—Children whose bodies have been overcome by accident or illness who must stay within the shelter of their homes are prospects.

Youth. Blessed is the church school which teaches and practices, "Remember now thy Creator in the days of thy youth." We are thinking about:

—The junior highs, 12-14. Here is the age where we make great gains or great losses. They very definitely are prospects.

—The seniors, 15-17. They are prospects.

—Those older youth, 18-21! But where are they? Gone to school and gone away from home? Yes, some. But many remain. They are prospects.

Adults. Some church schools have from one to twenty or more adult classes. But in other church schools adults have sometimes been overlooked. All church schools, however, should be thinking about:

—Young adults. They are from 22 (sometimes younger because of marriage or other responsibilities) to about 35. They are young homemakers. They are the backbone of many enterprises in the community. Often they have children who should be in church school. Too often they are not in church school. They are prospects.

—Mature adults who are use to carrying the responsibilities of home and work and community. They need the undergirding of Christian faith and teaching, and the church school needs them. They are prospects.

—Elderly people. Why should a person be denied the fellowship of a Sunday-school class and the solace of the Master's teaching just because old age has overtaken him? They are prospects.

—Shut-ins and the persons prevented for any reason from coming to the church building for regular sessions of the church school. The adult home roll is especially for them. They are prospects.

By prospects we mean individual people of all ages and conditions everywhere—the newcomers, the temporary residents, the overlooked ones, and the hard-to-get ones. The church school is for them all, and has something for each of them.

3. The idea of expending energy to increase membership is resisted by some on the grounds that attendance and participation are the important considerations, and membership is immaterial. Such a point of view is not to be encouraged. Attendance can hardly be cultivated effectively without some connection with or claim upon an individual. But even more than that is involved here. Membership signifies being a part of the enterprise far more than does attendance alone. We seek participation in the Christian educational part of the church's ministry on a stable and permanent basis. We seek participation from birth to death with as full involvement as is commensurate with the level of maturity and the talents of the individual. All of this implies membership. We are definitely seeking more persons to be members of the church school.

4. The remaining item to be considered under the heading, "What Do We Seek to Increase?" is attendance. We have taken a quick look at our purpose to increase the participation of individual persons in learning and practicing Christianity, to increase the church school, and to major on bringing about a "membership" relation which will have permanent significance. But without consistent attendance these three amount to little.

Need it be said again that the purpose in increasing attendance in the various parts of the church school (connection rather than attendance in home and extension service) rests on reasons more worthy than to set a record? The simple fact that intermittent attendance robs an individual of the benefits which await the regular attender should be enough to justify tremendous efforts in all church schools to bring attendance averages up. Fifty per cent is about the national average for the denominations taken as a whole.

At best there is far too little time available for Christian teaching. When poor attendance cuts that time in half, the consequences for the pupil are serious, and the efficiency of the enterprise is greatly curtailed. Church and church-school buildings and equipment have one of the lowest use rates of any enterprise in the community. Vast resources of the denomination in curriculum development, the work of the teacher or leader in preparation, the monetary investment in the physical plant, and many other factors focus on the pupil. They exist solely for him. If his utilization of them is haphazard, we are impelled for his sake to search for ways to improve the situation. Increasing average attendance is a sacred duty.

The Membership Cultivation Superintendent

Why Have One?

Experience supports the suggestion that in every church school there be an officer whose responsibility it is to lead in church-school membership and attendance increase. We call him membership cultivation superintendent.

It can be argued that if the members of the church school are vital, evangelical Christians increase in members and participation will take place without any particular plans to bring it about. Of course the same can be said about church membership. Certainly we can go along with this point of view as far as recognizing that quality of program and quality of membership take priority over procedural matters. But in today's world the definite fixing of responsibility to bring about desirable results is amply justified.

It can also be contended that responsibility for securing new members and improved attendance is part of the work of all officers and teachers, so why bother with a special leader for this purpose? Yet the success of church schools which have an active and able membership cultivation superintendent makes clear the wisdom of having this officer.

How Secured?

The simple answer is: In the same way you secure your other general officers. When electing the church-school superintendent, the division superintendents, and the other general officers, elect also a membership cultivation superintendent.

His Work

The specific responsibilities of some workers in the church school are unavoidably vague. Not so with the membership cultivation superintendent. His work can be clearly and precisely stated. It is to bring about continued increases in church-school membership and attendance. His work may not be easy to accomplish, but it is easy to understand.

Well-kept records reveal progress, or lack of it, and give clues to procedure in achieving increases. The membership cultivation superintendent and the secretarial force throughout the school must maintain close working relations. He and his workers must continually study the records and know what is happening in all parts of the school.

The Workers Associated with Him

He does not work alone. Although responsibility for success rests upon him, he is in effect the leader of a group of membership workers representing the various parts of the school. Together they form a team, working to increase membership and attendance.

In most schools the persons who will work with him are already at work on membership. They are known in their classes or groups as the membership committee, membership chairmen, or by other titles. It is not recommended that he try to arrange for a new set of membership workers but instead bring together into a team those already on the job. He should discover who these membership workers are in all classes and departments throughout the school. If he finds that important sections of the church school do not have membership workers already on the job, he will encourage their selection so that all major elements in the church school are represented in his team of workers.

In the very smallest schools he would have at least three membership workers associated with him, one each representing children's work, youth work, and adult work. In large schools the group of membership workers could be quite large if all departments and all adult classes were represented.

He brings all membership workers together for the purpose of developing plans for membership and attendance increase as outlined below. They should meet occasionally to discuss their work and develop their procedures. The membership cultivation superintendent serves as chairman and leader.

Although he is the responsible officer in the field of increasing church-school membership and attendance, he nevertheless must work in co-operation with the church-school superintendent, pastor, director or minister of Christian education (where there is one), and the other leaders. Nothing less than complete helpfulness on the part of all leaders will bring success, and that calls for understanding and co-operation.

It likewise is true that the whole membership of the church school and of the congregation should understand and co-operate with those bringing about membership and attendance increases in the church school. The membership cultivation superintendent should undertake to insure such understanding and co-operation.

His Relationship to the Commissions

The membership cultivation superintendent and his team of membership workers from the classes and departments work out plans for bringing about continued increase in membership and attendance. He takes these plans to the commission on education at least annually for discussion and approval. It is to be remembered that this work is under the commission on education. He and his workers administer the approved plans, working in harmony with the church-school superintendent and the other leaders and enlisting the co-operation of the congregation.

Here a distinction is to be noted: the membership cultivation superintendent and his workers are responsible for *church-school* membership and attendance. On the other hand the commission on membership and evangelism is responsible for *church* membership. This distinction has significance. In recruiting for church membership the commission on membership and evangelism works to secure a definite commitment to Christ. Also, the assumption of the vows of the church are involved. But in recruiting for church-school membership no commitment is asked of the individual.

There is thus clear differentiation between the two fields of responsibility. Yet there should be full co-operation and mutual helpfulness. And, of course, the ultimate goals are the same.

Procedures in Membership Increase

A Look at Modern Man

With the membership workers designated in each department or group and with a membership cultivation superintendent to lead them, how do they go about doing their work? Where do they catch hold? What specific items would be included in "a year's plan for membership and attendance increase" to be submitted to the commission on education for approval? Fortunately, the accumulated experience of successful, growing church schools suggests some answers to these questions.

The first one is a bit odd. It can hardly be included in an action program because it is primarily an attitude. Stated briefly, it is this: alertness to evaluate, to test, to ponder, in order that the procedures used to increase membership and attendance, will work in this modern day. This needs to be explained.

In varying degrees sociologists and the whole group of behavioral scientists are telling us that people today "are different." There is much to support the idea that persons born after World War II differ in many important respects from the older generation. The world in which they live certainly is different. Background, attitudes, standards of conduct, basic beliefs, spiritual values, factors making for credulity and skepticism —the whole array of whatever it is that provides guidance for persons is involved. Those who undertake to bring persons into the church school have always encountered inertia, preference for another way of life, and evasions of various sorts. But now a bland "Why should I?" is commonplace.

Not always is that skepticism based on irreligion. Frequently it is occasioned by disapproval of the church. Because of its partial inability to guide mankind in days of crucial change, the church is thought to have failed. Some with zeal for social change are impatient with the church's conservatism. Some with conservative learnings are impatient with the church's liberal position. We are in a badly mixed-up world. All this is reflected in church-school membership and attendance.

In this situation three suggestions are offered: (a) We are in the midst of discussing specific, detailed steps recommended for reaching more persons through the church school. They constitute a well thought-out, total plan and are validated in experience. But they should not be taken over bodily without thoughtful consideration. Will they work in your community? Will they apply equally for different age groups? Should some be used and others changed? (b) Do not be concerned over difficulties that do not exist. Not every teen-ager will try to stop you in your tracks with a sophisticated "Why?" And not every adult is a mixed up victim of a disordered world. (c) Honest enthusiasm, based on intelligent understandings and backed by good Christian example, still wins.

Developing True Concern

"Want to" is a priceless ingredient in a church school's plans for membership and attendance increase. It is more important than "know how." It has been said truly and repeatedly that "any church school can increase its membership and attendance if it really wants to and will work at it." Concern for doing this must exist throughout the congregation if the highest level of success is to be reached. How can true concern be developed?

In varying degrees concern for church-school increase already exists in most congregations. Often this is an uninformed concern and rests lightly on many individuals in the congregation. And unfortunately an increase in intelligent concern cannot be achieved by pressing a button. But it can be achieved.

Consider the part to be played by prayer. Among Christians the efficacy of prayer does not have to be argued. But sometimes prayer does have to be encouraged. Leaders setting about to increase an informed concern for the church school's growth will find themselves far along with their task if, as individuals and as a group, they have made prayer the basic element in their procedure. Where this has been done sincerely there is no question as to their dependence on the Holy Spirit. Without this dependence nothing of spiritual consequence is apt to happen.

Concern should be intelligent. On an average do the members of the congregation understand the purpose, the nature, and the scope of the church school? Unfortunately many otherwise informed churchmen think of it as being the Sunday school they knew as children, and primarily for children. These misconceptions need to be corrected if concern is to be intelligent, and they can be corrected through informational procedures open to us, as suggested below.

For instance, information concerning the church school can be an important part of a "know your church" program. A series of presentations can be arranged using different approaches such as church night, Sunday evening fellowship, sermons, leaflets, letters, three-minute talks at the Sunday morning church worship service. Or during a period of special emphasis carefully prepared statements can be made at the meetings of various organizations of the church. If there is a will to do it, the whole congregation can be informed concerning the church school and its vital importance.

But deep concern does not always result from information alone. Motivation can be a difficult and complicated matter. Developing true concern that through the church school more persons be reached, will undoubtedly require more than a program series on the purpose, the nature, and the scope of the church school. Hence the following additional suggestions:

Over a period of time what is said, or not said, from the pulpit can have vast influence on the congregation. A pastor truly concerned that the church school increase in effectiveness can transmit that concern to his people. Sermons on the "great commission" to teach and continued appreciative references to the work of the church school can greatly affect the situation for good.

Purposeful visiting in the homes of the congregation can carry the message of the desirability of outreach with the church-school program.

Again, concern is contagious. If a teacher or a parent or a member of the commission on education is himself sufficiently concerned to take time to visit others in the congregation to discuss the importance of the church school, that concern is very likely to be caught in some degree by those visited. This is time and energy consuming. Not many persons are willing to do such visiting. It depends on how much "want to" there is among the church-school workers. But if done intelligently and sincerely, it certainly works.

Posters and other visual reminders can do much to develop concern in the congregation. It is suggested that a consistently developed series will get better results than an incidental or casual approach. Films and filmstrips help, of course.

Much time must be spent with the workers on the detailed procedures involved in getting new members and in stimulating more regular attendance. This is necessary. But even if it means reducing somewhat the attention paid to procedure, spend time on the "why" as well as the "how." Even faithful officers and teachers often lack motivation in the matter of working for increases. Well-planned programs at workers' conference will help change this.

But before mentioning any of these suggestions, ask the commission on education this question, "How can we get the congregation really to want to increase church-school membership and attendance, and how can we get persons truly interested?" Ask the question sincerely and challengingly, be carefully prepared to contribute to the discussion, and see what proposals result.

Setting Goals

The development among leaders and the congregation as a whole of true concern to reach more persons with Christian teaching can normally lead to the question, "How far are we going to try to go?"

Not every church school will consider it helpful to include the setting of goals in its list of procedures for increasing membership and attendance. But the idea is so widely accepted as helpful that consideration of it seems appropriate here. When undertaken seriously such consideration will involve long range as well as more immediate goals.

Long-range goals for increase can usually best be originated in the commission on education and shared with the workers' conference and certainly with the official board. They should emerge as the result of thinking ahead for a period of years. Somewhere along their line of development they will inevitably become involved with long-range planning for increase in church membership and perhaps physical facilities. Foreseeable population trends, anticipated changes in the community, and the expected success of long-range plans for leadership development will be factors in long-range planning. But faith, too, will have a part. And often an arbitrary decision to increase by a certain amount every year over a period of time, regardless of what may be encountered, proves to be thoroughly warranted. Indeed, the church is being true to its real nature when it overcomes environing conditions instead of being overcome by them.

Short-range goals are important too. They can involve more persons in their planning and in their accomplishment. And they provide opportunity for frequent and illuminating checks and evaluations. A few basic considerations should be in mind when undertaking short-range goal-setting:

—The goals are people, not figures, or lines on a graph, or the exhilaration of success. When attention is fixed steadily on bringing actual persons into contact with the teachings and the person of the Master, goal-setting and accomplishment become *spiritual* matters.

—Challenge and faith are old, well-worn words. Be sure, though, that both are involved in your goal-setting process. Has there been sufficient prayer, sufficient knowledge and concern over lost and unreached persons, sufficient impact of Christ's dependence on us, to constitute a challenge in the deepest sense? If not, you are not ready to set goals. And is healthy Christian faith undergirding the whole matter?

—Involve in goal-setting the persons who will be responsible for achieving them. Does this idea have to be defended in your church? It is of basic importance.

—If each class and group can share in the spirit of the matter and determine definitely what it will purpose to do, the goals for the whole church school can be the sum of the separate goals of classes and groups. Both membership and attendance should figure in the plans.

—Involve all parts of the church school in the goals (Sunday school, Sunday evening fellowship, weekday activities, and home and extension service) and all age groups.

—Co-operation in goals that may have been established for the district in which the church school is located must, of course, be in mind.

—Goals should be clear and understood, they should be recorded, they should be made public and be displayed as continual reminders.

—Short-range goals involve a short period of time. Consider the advantage, however, of a moving or continuing goal that includes specific periods of time but contemplates another and another and another, as periods are covered and evaluations made. Short-range goals for a brief period only, as

61

in a campaign, may be justified in certain instances. But goals for continued growth are more constructive and more valid in the light of our continuing mission.

—Available space and available teachers and leaders must be in mind if goal-setting is to be intelligently done. But smaller goals because of shortage either of space or leadership is tragic. Courageous Christian procedure is not to limit outreach because of limitations but rather to correct the limitations of space and leadership. Wise goal-setting may serve to emphasize the need for space and leaders and to speed correction. Carry forward both the outreach and the correction.

—The only type of "contest" which merits approval is competition with one's own former record. To do better than we did last time is worthy. To do better than our friends in another group is questionable motivation.

—A special service of commitment and consecration should be held to present to God the high purposing of the church school and to assume obligation to fulfill it.

Policy Decisions

At the outset certain policy decisions should be made.

Will the source for prospective new members primarily be within the local church and the church family? Or will the church school search for persons not connected with the church? Or both?

It is important that the decision be to do both. And this decision should be made by the commission on education and administered by the membership cultivation superintendent and his fellow workers. In large schools it frequently transpires that there is no common understanding at this point. The plan of recruiting new church-school members from those already reached in one way or another by the church is followed exclusively by some classes and groups. While this source is of great importance and should be diligently worked, if there is no seeking beyond this, one of the greatest opportunities for evangelistic outreach which the church has is lost.

Assuming that this double approach will be followed, it will prove helpful if under the supervision of the membership cultivation superintendent a continuing record be kept of new church-school members with respect to this matter. If over a period of time new members are not coming from both of these sources, corrective steps should be taken.

In considering specific sources and ways of finding prospective new members for the church school it does not prove practical to set up two lists, that is, one for recruiting persons already connected with the church in some way and another for persons who have no connection with the church or any of its organizations. The reason it is not practical is that often a particular procedure will yield prospects from both groups. There can, however, be times when efforts are focused on one or the other as there is need. The importance of this is so great that it should not be allowed to fade from continuing plans of the membership cultivation superintendent and his membership workers.

A second policy decision relates to parish boundaries.

If our purpose were only to find a few new members now and then when stimulated by a passing campaign or sporadic effort, there would be scant reason to be concerned over the geographical territory to be worked. But surely our purpose is more sturdy than that. The membership cultivation superintendent and his membership workers are permanent officials with continuing responsibility. Within what geographical boundaries, then, are they to work?

Often this question cannot be answered by the officials involved, or even by the commission on education, though the commission on education should face it and continue with the question until it is answered. With the possible exception of the establishment of outpost church schools, to be discussed later, the parish of the church school and of the church are identical. But what is the parish of the church?

Frequently this question must be taken to the district authorities. Occasionally a district can neatly be divided among the churches which compose it and every square foot assigned to a particular church. But usually the solution is not that simple. Downtown churches often, by agreement, have territories overlapping suburban churches, and town churches have membership extending to the neighborhood of rural churches.

But the matter should be faced and a definite position reached. The membership cultivation superintendent and his workers should know positively whether they are operating under geographical limitations and if so, what their specific territory is.

Then they should realize that every prospective new member for the church school who resides within that territory is their responsibility. Their plans should be ultimately to reach every one.

A third policy decision concerns interrelationships among recruiting members for the church, and members for other organizations within the church.

Theoretically, one completely centralized approach to all membership recruiting throughout the whole church seems to have value. In practice, though, it leaves much to be desired. Even with a proper assignment of administrative responsibility and sound planning to get the job done, it is still true that zeal on the part of individual members to secure more members is a basic ingredient for success. Said another way, new membership recruiting must be kept close to the members themselves, and individual organizations or groups with which the new member will be connected must themselves also be directly involved and feel a sense of responsibility.

Fortunately this can be true without adversely affecting the very desirable sense of unity throughout the church and its organizations. Nor need it compromise our fundamental position that the church school is the church as the church engages in its teaching function.

Everything considered, the proposal to have a plan for recruiting members for the church school, as such, is felt to be sound. It is proper also for the woman's society, and other organizations within the church, as well as for the church itself. But that does not mean that no relationship should exist among them or that there should not be co-operation and mutual helpfulness.

It is suggested that the practical basis for policy decisions in this matter is separate endeavors for membership recruiting for the church itself, for the church school, and for the other church organizations, but such co-operation and interdependence among all recruiters as results in each having all others in mind and each working for all others. Specifically, the membership cultivation superintendent in the church school and the membership workers associated with him have only two chief responsibilities, namely, to lead the church school in (a) increasing church-school membership, and (b) increasing attendance (at Sunday school, at Sunday evening fellowship, and at weekday activities). Yet in discharging this responsibility they will be alert to guide persons into the membership of other groups and the church itself as opportunity presents itself. Certainly it is true that in guiding persons and families to assume vows of church membership there should be active zeal on the part of the workers who are making the contact to bring those persons—all of them—into membership in the church school, and, as appropriate, into the woman's society, the men's organization, and so on. And recruiters for new members in the church school should be equally alert to co-operate in the same way.

Summarizing: It is suggested that the church school should have its own organization and plans for membership increase. But all church-school membership workers should work also for membership increase in the church and all church organizations and co-operate with the membership workers of all other church organizations.

Finding Prospective Members

It is reported that the county organization of a denomination noted for its church-school activity maintains a card file with pertinent facts on every person in the county, and it keeps the file up to date. A tremendous undertaking! That denomination is probably the fastest growing in the county. There may be a number of reasons for their growth, but one reason certainly is that *they know their constituency.* They know who and where their prospective new members are—all of them.

That is one way of doing it.

But for most denominations and quite certainly for a local church school, simpler and yet effective ways are needed to find prospective new church-school members. Fortunately we have at our disposal an accumulation of experience-proven ways to go about it. Certain of these are listed for your consideration:

Where can prospects be found?

1. *From your church roll.*

a) Go through your complete church roll, name by name, check with your church-school roll and list all who are not members of your church school.

b) Pick up names from your church families, thus: arrange the names on the church roll by families. Copy these names onto a large card, a card for a family, and add names of all other members of that family. Show approximate ages. Then check these complete family lists with your church-school roll.

2. *By listing from memory.*

In the various groups and organizations of the church distribute blank cards and pencils. Ask for the names and addresses of persons who should be in your church school. Do this in:

> general assemblies of the church school
> Sunday-school classes
> Sunday-evening groups
> official board meetings
> meetings of woman's society
> regular church services

3. *From organization rolls.*

Go over the rolls of the various organizations of the church, such as woman's society, men's clubs, church boards and committees (including the official board), and list persons who are not members of the church school.

4. *From community statistics.*

The bureau of vital statistics for the community and connections with hospitals and physicians will yield information concerning newborn babies for the nursery roll. Continual emphasis in the various organizations of the church, such as woman's society, mothers' clubs and classes, will encourage the practice of reporting births. By checking public-school rolls and public utility customer lists new families and new persons will be discovered.

5. *By making a survey.*

The community survey calls for visiting every dwelling and securing data, just as is done with the government census. This is by far the most thoroughgoing and satisfactory method of finding prospects, if well handled. It should be done by competent people who understand what they are doing. It should be done in such a way as to meet the survey needs for all phases of the local church. Interchurch and interdenominational surveys are preferred in many communities.

Here are steps necessary for a successful survey. They should be modified at any points necessary to allow the full and equal participation of other groups, whenever other church groups are also involved.

a) Appoint a survey committee. This can be the commission on education itself, or a subcommittee. The membership cultivation superintendent may well serve as the chairman of this committee. Its membership includes, along with others you may want, the age group membership workers, the church-school superintendent, and the pastor. Its work is to plan the survey in all its details.

b) Make a policy as to how often there should be a survey. The best arrangement for most churches is to have a survey once a year, with provision to keep it up-to-date between surveys. Do not have a survey as a single, independent event. Think of the survey as part of your continuing search for people who should be in church school, and plan accordingly.

c) Decide on the exact territory to be covered. If you do not know the exact territory for which your church is responsible and you cannot find out, make the best decision you can and go ahead. If in open country, use highways, rivers, railroads, or other recognized boundaries. If in town or city, use streets. Make it clear whether one side or both sides of the boundary highway or street are included.

d) Subdivide the territory into "survey units," each including the amount of territory one team or individual can work in the time decided on for the survey. If the territory is large, group the "survey units" into districts or zones.

e) Make maps. This is not hard. It does not require expert ability. A map for almost every community is available from some source. Make enlarged portions of the map to cover the territory being surveyed. Each "survey unit" should have its own map, sufficiently enlarged to give all needed detail. All maps should be prepared in advance of the survey.

f) Decide on the date for the survey, the time of day, and the length of time in which you will try to complete it. Sunday afternoon is often best, with dinner at the church so the workers can get started on time. Of course it will often be necessary to go back to some places a second time because of persons being away, but it is usually much better to complete the bulk of the survey at one time. The practice of giving out cards and territory assignment with the request that work be completed "within the next few days" is not recommended.

g) Secure workers early. You will need two workers for each "survey unit" into which you have divided your territory because it is advisable to work in pairs. For a large survey division leaders will be needed in addition. The members of the planning committee may serve as survey workers. The age of the workers is not important—from high school to middle age and beyond is your range. The important things are (1) intelligence to comprehend what is involved, (2) consecration to represent the Christian enterprise, (3) personality to create a favorable impression, (4) dependability to insure the work being done. Ask each class or department to furnish its quota of workers. Announce from the pulpit. Create an atmosphere of expectancy and approval for the survey. As far as possible select your workers rather than depend upon volunteers.

h) Avoid duplication by making the survey cover the needs of all groups in the church needing the information it will yield. If any group in addition to the church school is interested, invite them to co-operate and to have representatives on the survey committee. Likewise, if other denominations in the community are planning a survey, *it is often better to combine forces and conduct the survey interdenominationally* than to have each denomination make a separate survey covering the same territory. But be sure all plans are understood and agreed to by all, and that it is decided in advance exactly how the information gained by the survey is to be divided and how the cards are to be handled. It is advisable to have these agreements in writing.

i) Assure transportation for the survey workers if they do not have their own.

j) Instruct every worker at a meeting held for that purpose. If the workers have dinner at the church on Sunday before making the survey Sunday afternoon, the instruction meeting should be held immediately after dinner before the workers go out for the survey. The leader of the meeting should prepare carefully, have all materials ready, and have all plans worked out in advance. He should also inspire the workers with the importance of the survey in the work of the Master. The following simple instructions should be given. There should be opportunity for questions. Demonstration through a role play of a visit will be helpful.

(1) Understand that this is a Christian enterprise for the promotion of Christ's kingdom, and that courteous, friendly interest in the persons you see will help greatly. Encourage and instruct every worker to make each visit yield the greatest possible results. Many times genuine interest in church-school attendance can be won during the survey worker's visit.

(2) Check your supplies to see that you have pencil or pen, a sufficient number of survey cards, envelopes in which to keep them, and a clear statement of the exact territory you are to cover.

(3) Visit every home or place where people reside, without any exceptions. Do this even though you may think you already have all the information, and even though the persons in the home are known to be church people. Make the survey complete.

(4) Fill out the card completely and accurately. Any blank spaces will mean incomplete information. Do not put on the card the names of persons not living at that address, even though they may be members of the family. Do include members of the family who are away temporarily, indicating on the card when they are expected to return. In the case of more than one family at one address, use separate cards, but note on each card that there is another family at that address, giving the name. In the case of persons not living in a family, use a card for each.

(5) Write legibly. Write "Mrs." before names of all married women. Indicate sex because the name does not always indicate.

(6) Work your territory completely. Stay within your own territory.

(7) Do your work promptly and within the time allotted if possible. Report to your chairman for instructions if at any address you were unable to get full information.

(8) Return your envelope and all cards promptly to the designated person at the designated place and time.

k) Conserve results by planning in complete detail what will be done with the cards and the information they carry. Have these plans written down in full and agreed to in advance. The following should be included in the plan:

(1) Require all cards to be turned in to a designated person at designated time and place.

(2) Sort cards by denominational preference. Do this in the following way: If *all* the names on a card indicate a preference for a denomination, turn that card over to that denomination. If more than one denominational preference is indicated on one card, make duplicate copies of the card and handle as above.

(3) Arrange cards alphabetically by family names.

(4) Check all names with church school roll and plainly mark all who are not members of the church school.

(5) Copy into the church school prospect book the names of all persons indicating denominational preference or no preference, who are not now members of the church school.

(6) If the church school alone is taking the survey, the survey cards themselves (after being copied into the prospect book) can be given to the membership workers who are to follow them up. But if other groups in the church are co-operating in the survey, making it impractical to release the survey cards, then church-school prospect assignment cards should be made out from the prospect book and given to the workers. In case prospects of more than one age group (children, youth, or adult) appear on the same card, give to a family worker. If card contains prospects of only one age group, give to a worker responsible for that age.

(7) The church-school prospect assignment card is to be returned finally to the person designated for this purpose, with a report on each prospect. This is, after the complete work of follow-up has been done and the case closed one way or the other. The report will be posted in the prospect book.

Prospects Becoming Members

We face now the all important matter of making members out of prospects. Two necessary steps are suggested: assigning prospects to workers, and contacting the prospect in such a way that he becomes a member.

Little need be said concerning assigning prospects to workers beyond the statement itself, but that little has basic importance. Because every prospect is a person, an immortal soul, there should be Christian concern for each one of them. That is why each one should be recorded in some way (we suggest in a prospect book), and when assigned to a worker for follow-up the record should show to whom assigned and when. The worker receiving the assignment should report the outcome—success or failure, and if failure, why and what next steps are suggested.

Lack of initial success should not be cause for dropping a prospect. Indeed, under the guidance of the membership cultivation superintendent a reasonable procedure should be established and followed when a worker does not report success. The "workers," of course, are the membership workers from each major group in the church school who are associated with the membership cultivation superintendent as discussed beginning on p. 55.

Assignments, naturally, are made in terms of the appropriateness of the prospect becoming a member of the particular group which the worker represents. If families or persons of different age groups closely associated are prospects, assignments to workers can well cut across age lines and the family or group be contacted together. For handling situations of this kind, which are common, a practical procedure should be agreed upon by the membership cultivation superintendent and the workers.

Contacting the prospect in such a way that he becomes a member calls for the most intelligent procedure possible. If the prospect does not become a member, all that has taken place up to this point has been in vain and a person who needs what the church school can provide will not receive it. Church schools that have been successful report the following:

1. When a prospect is to be gotten in, a personal visit is best. Two workers in a team usually are better than one working alone. Sometimes three can work together profitably. Eager workers, trained and capable, making personal visits constitute the most fruitful method.

2. Writing personal letters to prospects is often a good method. It is not usually as effective as a visit. To supplement a visit it is splendid.

3. A phone call to the prospect is not usually as good as a visit.

4. Periods of special emphasis can yield good results:

a) Periodic or seasonal emphases on getting new members are highly desirable, if properly conducted. But they should not take the place of the steady week-after-week and month-after-month work of getting new members as a normal and regular part of the program of the church school.

b) The special emphasis should not be a "desperate expedient," resorted to because matters have been allowed to drift. It should be a normal and a regular part of the year-round plan for getting new members.

5. Training of membership workers.

a) The effort expended on increasing the zeal and devotion of a membership worker makes a contribution to his training because much of this work comes from the heart.

b) Training will include attention to the element of personal influence, tact, graciousness, a sense of the appropriate, accommodation to the age and circumstances of the prospect.

c) Training will include knowledge of the aims, organization, equipment, leadership personnel, and curriculum of the church school.

d) Training will include information on such subjects as these:

—When it is best to send only one person to see a prospect, and when best to go in teams. As a rule, two membership workers visiting together can accomplish more than two workers visiting separately.

—Making arrangements in advance to see the prospect, or considering the limited circumstances under which telephoning or writing may be substituted for visiting.

—When to ask for assistance, as from the superintendent or the pastor.

—What facts discovered through the contact should be passed on to the pastor or others.

—The fact that the membership worker inevitably represents not only the church school but the church and religion in general, and that much depends upon the impression he makes.

—A direct, cheerful presentation of the subject, in a natural way, is better than an indirect or casual approach. The subject is worthy and deserves a hearty and forthright presentation. Cordiality and great personal interest are indispensable. Neither bruskness nor an apologetic manner will win.

—Study each prospect with care before making contact. Know the family situation and the personality of the prospect if at all possible.

—Where transportation to and from the church school is a problem, give advance consideration and have a solution ready if possible.

Keeping Interest High

The remaining basic suggestion to church schools undertaking a serious program of membership increase is to keep interest high.

Having a membership cultivation superintendent and a group of membership workers, permanently assigned to this task and actively at work, is in itself an important factor in maintaining interest on the part of all.

In the commission on education a permanent committee on increasing membership and attendance, with active leadership and called upon frequently to report progress, will serve to keep the subject in focus for the entire membership of the commission.

Reasonably frequent programs and a brief report at every session of the workers' conference, reports to the official board, paragraphs in the church bulletin, posters and displays, all help in maintaining interest in church-school membership and attendance increase. Favorable comment from the pulpit is invaluable. Indeed, the suggestions on developing concern (p. 58) all can serve this purpose also.

Adequate and attractive displays of the goals toward which the church school is working will assist. Graphs posted each week showing progress for the church school as a whole are effective, and individual charts and graphs in classrooms and group meeting places are recommended.

Perhaps the heart of the matter, though, will be found to be in the fine Christian zeal of earnest disciples who are thoroughly convinced that every possible person, young and old, should be gotten into church school where the way of the Master is taught. True interest in church-school membership and attendance increase stems from true Christian concern for bringing people to Christ.

Procedures in Increasing Attendance

The Importance of Quality in What Is Offered

Regrettably, the importance of quality needs to be established. Far too frequently one encounters church schools where conscientious and often well-planned effort is being made to increase average attendance, with no thought given to the factor which can cancel all efforts, that is, the rank inferiority of teaching and general surroundings. We cannot agree with those who feel that good teaching and appropriate general surroundings will automatically insure high average attendance. Neither can we agree with those who would depend solely on direct cultivation procedures. Plain honesty demands that there be something worth attending. Good sense demands it too. Along with a direct approach to increasing attendance must be that which will insure high quality in what is offered those who do attend.

Friendliness and Fellowship

Regardless of size, condition, or location, there is one thing in which every church school can excel if it wants to, that is in being friendly and hospitable. True hospitality roots deeply in the friendly nature of the Christian. A measure of the genuineness of a church school's religion is the quality of its hospitality. Hospitality pays big dividends in increased average attendance. As a gilt-edge investment consider the following:

—A hospitality committee that takes its job seriously and keeps everlastingly at it.
—Greeters at all doors. Use adults, youth, and children as greeters. Coach greeters in friendliness.
—Letters. Letters of welcome to new pupils. Letters of sympathy. Letters of congratulations. Letters on all important occasions.
—Hospitality workers in every class and group.

72

—Sponsors for new members, who will extend every possible courtesy and encouragement.

—Such an interpretation of Christianity as will cause all members to be kind and friendly to everyone else.

Some centuries ago the Reverend Mr. Sterne announced a splendid formula that applies to increasing attendance:

> Hail, ye small, sweet courtesies of life,
> How smooth do ye make the road of it.

Involvement and Participation

We have a built-in attendance stimulator when pupils are so skillfully involved in the work that they become true participants in the fellowship of their groups. This may need a little explaining.

Drop in on a class of older children, youth, or adults some Sunday morning. In many classes the only active person in the room is the teacher. Everyone else is passive. Except for the secretary, no one but the teacher carries any responsibility. Everyone else just sits. There is no "built-in attendance stimulator" here. This unpromising situation can be partly salvaged, though, if the program of the group is not limited to what you observed when you dropped in. If there is a service program under way, for instance, members of the class can be involved in it.

But far better is the approach to Christian education which from the outset is planned to include pupils (of all ages) with the teachers or leaders in the teaching and the learning activities. Pupil participation is achieved these days in many ways (see p. 84). Here we find those "built-in" qualities which interest and involve the pupil so that attendance occurs because of genuine desire to be there.

True involvement can result from (a) a sense of discipleship which keeps the pupil loyal and present regardless, (b) assuming responsibility such as holding office from which satisfactions are gained, and (c) a teaching-learning procedure which from its very nature makes the pupil a participant just as definitely as it does the teacher.

But regardless of how participation is achieved, it is a powerful factor in stimulating attendance.

An Action Program

The membership cultivation superintendent and the workers associated with him have two direct approaches to increasing average attendance. One is to follow up every absence. The other is to attack the causes of absence. If these two things are done intelligently and faithfully *attendance will increase!*

Help all teachers and leaders to see the importance of *following up every absence.* Here is one of our greatest points of failure. The grave consequences of neglected absences must be realized. Discuss this in the commission on education and the workers' conference. Make it a major matter in all planning groups. Our first consideration in the matter of following up absentees is to devote enough thought and effort to the matter to insure everyone being really concerned.

The development of a simple and practical plan for following up absences is necessary. This would include:

1. Taking note when absences occur. Simply marking the class book is not enough. Arrange to list absentees on cards. The secretary and a membership worker should be responsible for doing this listing.

2. Assigning the absentee to a membership worker. The responsibility for follow-up should be definitely fixed.

3. Visiting or telephoning the absentee and urging return.

4. Reporting on two things:

a) that contact was actually made with the absentee, and

b) the reason for the absence, if the reason was discovered.

Keeping the plan in force is a continuing problem. But that is true of all phases of church-school work. It will require constant vigilance.

It has been said by a wise church-school leader, "People can't resist attention." That is true. You can depend upon the fact that if you will pay attention to people they will respond—not every one and not every time, but most of them will respond. It can be depended upon that if every absence is followed up in some intelligent way, attendance positively will increase.

Following up absences is *remedial.*

Attacking the causes of absence is *preventive.* A church school which discovers and does something about the causes of absence will increase attendance noticeably. But it will do more than that. It will vastly improve its work. In discovering things which need improvement, it will open up new avenues for Christian service to its members. The reports turned in by visitors who check on absentees will constitute a barometer of the school, and will provide the pastor and other officials with valuable information.

The membership cultivation superintendent and the membership workers should assume responsibility for discovering and thinking through whatever exists in their school and community that would contribute to irregular attendance. After getting the facts, the findings should be taken to the commission on education. In the commission steps can be taken to bring about remedies, using the regular channels of administration. It is not the responsibility of the membership cultivation superintendent and the membership workers to undertake the reforms that may be needed. If they did, they would be taking over the responsibilities of the superintendents, officers, and other leaders. But it is their responsibility to bring suggestions to the commission for its consideration and action.

Poor teaching probably heads the list of causes of absence which are within our control. Lack of hospitality will be a close second, with unattractive surroundings also high on the list.

Some causes of absence are beyond our control. Illness, unavoidable absence from the community, inescapable responsibilities which conflict as to time, are circumstances we can do little about. But sometimes absence is caused by indifference, or by social pressures of gang or group, or by antagonisms. Sometimes we can do something about these things through a carefully devised, long-range program in the community.

We should hesitate a long time before we say that a thing can't be done, if it is in the interest of the Lord's work.

What other causes of absence are there? The question is well worth careful thought and courageous action.

Establishing Outposts

What Do We Mean by an "Outpost"?

It's simple. It means doing business in more places than one. There often are persons within the area of a church's responsibility who, for one reason or another, will not come to that church. But they may attend a Sunday-school class or other group started in their neighborhood by that church. That is an outpost.

Why Establish Outposts?

Because it is a tested way to reach more people with the teachings of Christ. Not every church school should start an outpost. But multiplied thousands should. Are there people in your community who do not attend your church school because of social, cultural, or economic reasons who might attend classes of their own if you started such near them? If the answer is yes, you have your reason.

Here is one interesting possibility: Many times comity agreements assign locations before resources are available for a new church. In such situations the officials responsible for starting new churches often will welcome the co-operation of a nearby church school. By starting an outpost church school, sponsored by an existing church school, you can conduct an "advance operation." When the new church can be established you will already have the beginning of the congregation—the outpost church school.

Relationships

Of course you must clear with your district superintendent in order to be in harmony with church and church-school extension plans. And the pastor and official board must be in on the project. But the responsibility rests upon your commission on education. The outpost will be under the commission just as is your present church school. Until the new group gains strength and develops its own leadership, it will be served by the general officers of the parent church school. You simply will do business in two places.

Procedures

Here are the steps a Midwestern church school took in establishing an outpost:

—an area of opportunity was selected
—approval was secured
—sponsors were selected (a young adult class)
—detailed plans were made
—a meeting place was secured
—teachers were enlisted
—literature was ordered
—visits were made (to every home in the neighborhood) and members enrolled
—publicity was wisely developed
—the first session was well handled
—close relations were maintained
—plans were developed for eventual operation by leaders from the new group, with the sponsorship and basic relationship continuing.

Eventual Independence?

Perhaps yes. Perhaps no. In some situations the new establishment should continue as a sponsored outpost indefinitely. In any event, even though outpost status is permanent, the largest possible amount of leadership should come from the new group.

These additional thoughts concerning outposts: The denominations in America that are consistently growing are those that have consistently increased the number of local units from which they operate. A part of their formula for increasing church-school membership is to increase the number of their church schools. It is estimated that the United States population will reach 228,000,000 by 1975. At present only one American in four is a member of a church school. America needs more church schools—many, many more.

5

MATERIALS, TEACHING PROCEDURES, PROGRAM

Materials

From the standpoint of those who guide a church school the materials involved in the operation of the church school can be grouped in two classifications. One is the lesson materials—pupils' materials and teachers' helps. The other is guidance materials to help teachers and officers understand how to do their work.

Lesson Materials

The dominant pattern in American Protestantism is for a denomination to make available to its local church schools a variety of lesson materials from which choice can be made in terms of local needs and

78

differences in groups. This means that while those who prepare and publish the lesson materials do type them as to theology, biblical content, denominational slant, and general direction, it is also true that within the local church school those in charge must be able to make wise choices from what is offered by their denominational publisher.

To aid in doing this it is the usual practice for detailed descriptions to be available from the publishers. For instance, in The Methodist Church and booklet *Learners and Literature* carries a complete description of all the lesson and teaching material published by the denomination. The publication *Forecast* is especially helpful in describing and associating audio-visuals with specific lesson series as well as describing printed resources. The book *Outlines of Curriculum,* published annually, gives outline description of every lesson in every series for the year. It is an amazingly effective guide to quick understanding of what will be found in the various lesson materials and teaching helps. The booklet *Foundations of Christian Teaching in Methodist Churches* is a statement of "the assumptions of Christian education that underlie the philosophy of the curriculum." Equipped with these the leaders in the local church school can know accurately what is available, the presuppositions that have governed in its preparation, and how to select intelligently what is best for their church school, all approved materials and all within the range of the denomination's basic purposes. Check with your denominational publishers for this type of guidance.

But the production of pupils' and teachers' materials is not confined to denominational boards of education and their publishers. Many independent, commercial publishers operate in this field and continually advertise their product in competition with the denominational producers. The local church school is often faced with the question of using its own denominational materials exclusively or of turning in part, or wholly, to commercial producers (see p. 82).

Where this is the case there are factors which can aid in arriving at an intelligent decision:

1. *Denominational Loyalty.* Involved here is more than blind loyalty, virtuous and defensible though that may be. More, perhaps, than in any other way the church-school pupil learns about his own denomination from the materials he uses in church school. Responsible participation in the life of the church depends on accurate knowledge of the nature and program of the church. A whole generation of persons uninformed about a denomination's missionary program, its colleges and universities, its evangelical approach, its stewardship ideals, and its interpretation of theology can result from the use of materials from independent com-

mercial publishers. A church school which thinks it is exercising freedom in choosing commercially produced lesson materials actually is enslaving itself in a situation which shuts out its pupils from knowledge of its own denomination.

2. *Theology and Doctrine.* There are differences in point of view concerning theology and doctrine. Lesson material cannot be written in such a way as to avoid taking a stand on theology and doctrine. There can be no assurance that independent commercially produced materials will not conflict with the denomination's position in these matters. It is distressing to note situations in which what is taught in a class on Sunday morning undermines what the minister is preaching from his pulpit later that same morning.

3. *Educational Integrity.* There are shortcuts to lesson preparation and to teaching procedure. Some materials are easy to teach, others difficult. But their value to the development of Christians is not determined by whether they are easy or difficult. Indeed, good teaching is a difficult thing. Beware of "materials that teach themselves." As a matter of fact, beware of the approach that suggests the teaching of materials at all. The intent of the church school should be to teach persons, not materials. Teaching materials is easy. Teaching persons is hard.

In this matter of understanding lesson materials, those who guide the church school have the thrilling opportunity of pushing back horizons and stretching minds. Reflected in the lesson material is the basic approach to Christian education held by those who produced it. And reflected in the development of persons in a class is the basic approach to Christian education held by those who teach them. Here are two very different but commonly held points of view. Surely the second of these is to be preferred:

a) One approach is that there is a body of content to be learned, and when it is learned the process is complete. Certain facts concerning the Bible, the Bible content itself, items of doctrine and church history, the denominational position on morality and religious custom—these and other facts make up the content to be learned. Under this concept the church school is very much like the public school. When one reaches a certain degree of proficiency in mastering the factual material involved, he has completed the course and is through. Where this point of view is held it is seldom that there is provision for adults.

b) The other approach differs in two respects. One difference is that the final purpose is redemptive rather than informational. That is, the ultimate objective is lives changed toward Christ rather than merely to impart holy facts. Information, of course, is involved. Facts concerning the

Bible and the Christian Way are vitally necessary. But they are means to an end, not the end itself. Information about religious things is merely a necessary step toward the goal of a changed and redeemed life. The other difference applying to this second approach is that it involves people from birth to death. Christian education so conceived is for persons of all ages. Adults as well as children and youth find guidance and strength for daily living through continued church-school participation when this approach governs.

Regrettably, it must be recognized that there are many teachers whose approach conforms to a) above, rather than to b).

The amount of Bible in lesson materials likewise is a subject of misunderstanding, discussion, and sometimes grave dissention. Be it said that the biblical content of denominational lesson materials is higher than often realized. When complete biblical passages are printed in full in the materials, one gets the impression that there is fine Bible content. There it is to see and read. But when instead only the biblical reference is printed, with the intent that the pupil will go to his Bible for the detailed passage and thus add to his familiarity with his Bible, the impression often is that the materials lack in biblical content. Wise church-school administrators are alert to this situation, and are not led astray by it.

And be it also said that to achieve the purposes for which it exists a church school must be more than a Bible school. This is preliminary to consideration of a problem almost always encountered by those who guide our church schools: What should be our attitude toward those teachers who want to dispense with all lesson materials (pupils' materials and teachers' helps) and use only the Bible?

In answer it is suggested that the circumstances should determine the decision. At least two factors should be considered: (a) At the stage of development which the class represents, what is their need? Is, or is not, their need being met by the available lesson materials? Considering the all-around Christian growth desired, will it be best for the class to leave the regular materials for a time and "just study the Bible"? Occasionally it will be; often it will not be. (b) Is the teacher competent to teach "just the Bible"? Many teachers are; many are not.

This is such an important matter, and the Bible occupies such a central and hallowed place in Christian education that further explanation is in order.

Actually, it is impossible to teach "just the Bible." Inescapably, what is taught is someone's interpretation of the Bible—the teacher's interpretation or that of some commentator or other source of biblical information to which the teacher turns for help. But the plea often is made that there will be no interpretation, that the Bible will speak for itself. Actually, it is difficult to arrange such a situation except as an individual reads for himself alone. Interpretation begins to enter in the selection of passages to be studied. Interpretation certainly has entered when one reads passages aloud. The Twenty-third Psalm can be read aloud with certain words emphasized and one meaning results. It can be read aloud, but with the emphasis placed differently, and an entirely different meaning emerges.

So the question turns out to be "Whose interpretation of the Bible is most to be desired? Who is best able to interpret?" Seldom is the teacher as skilled in biblical knowledge as are the lesson writers.

This is not to suggest that it is unwise for an individual to study the Bible itself, just for itself, and on occasion with no commentary. It is merely to suggest that those responsible for guiding the church school should understand the factors that operate when Bible study goes forward under the guidance of the writers who prepare the lesson materials, and that operate when an individual teacher takes over instead.

Before concluding the consideration of lesson materials from the point of view of those responsible for guiding a church school, note should be taken of the assigning of responsibility for selecting and ordering those materials. Who makes the decisions as to what materials will be used? Who orders it? Who has custody of it and arranges its distribution? Quite obviously no answer is universally applicable.

But in the matter of who decides what lesson materials shall be used, there can be a specific recommendation. It is that this responsibility should be lodged with the commission on education. This is true even in the light of the fact that in general the official board is a more authoritative body in the local church. The lesson materials are so involved in the deeper developments of the church school and selection of the materials so vital, that their selection should be the clear responsibility of the body responsible for the operation of the church school. And, of course, selection should be within the options provided by the denomination.

There are a number of alternatives but they usually lead to difficulty. To allow individual teachers to choose the materials they want to use negates orderly progress and pupil development, lowers standards, and soon results in chaos. For the official board to take over denies the ability and the authority of the commission on education and often gets the official board involved in matters well beyond its depth.

Good practice also seems to favor having a literature secretary who, under the direction of the commission on education, does the secretarial work involved in ordering the lesson materials. Many church schools have found it wise to have the orders approved by the commission before they become valid. There is ample experience to justify the suggestion that the selection, the ordering, and the utilization of lesson materials all be under the immediate control of the commission on education.

Guidance Materials

By guidance material, as distinguished from lesson material, we mean materials to help teachers and officers understand how to do their work. These materials, too, consist of audio-visuals as well as printed items.

This phase of the matter can be quickly covered. Interestingly enough, church schools that would not dream of trying to operate without lesson materials often go on from year to year depending upon the native skills of leaders, with scant attention given the excellent manuals, pamphlets, audio-visuals, and articles in church-school periodicals, painstakingly gotten together to help them be more effective workmen. Many books in this field are issued every year, but their total circulation hardly makes a dent on their market. It is a simple matter to write to your general board of education for catalogs of manuals and booklets and list of books backed by experience and written just to help you do a better job. It will be rewarding.

Teaching Procedures

It is not required that those who guide a church school be trained experts in the art of teaching. But it is highly desirable that they understand the basic factors, in so far as they are known, which characterize good teaching procedures in order that there be good teaching throughout the school. The corollary, of course, is that they likewise should understand how to bring about the good teaching procedures which their understanding calls for.

What are the basic factors?

Uncertainty

Uncertainty is a factor encountered sooner or later if the inquiry is realistic and all are extensive. Despite real progress in understanding the processes of the mind, the limits of our present knowledge are reached uncomfortably soon. What is known about how to get through to the mind, to make things stick in the mind, and, more important, how to supply the mind with data to grind on (and the will to grind) as it moves to new creative levels seems quite imposing. But far too often we suddenly find ourselves out at first base instead of making a home run. In spite of progress we still know far too little even about the transmitting and use of facts.

But the really hard going is found in the realm of attitudes. Using modern procedures we may think that we are doing splendidly in guiding the development of fine, virtuous attitudes, and may think we are quite the masters of the situation. Then along comes an unexpected prejudice and torpedoes the whole structure.

This general problem of the best known procedures not guaranteeing success is not new. Parents have long been aware of it. Two children in the same family, under the same circumstances, often turn out very differently. Modern education has made commendable progress but has by no means solved all its problems.

Any attempt to discuss teaching procedures should be well fortified with humility.

Targets

Some decades back one was expected to take sides in the controversy over whether Christian education should be content-centered or life-centered, that is, whether the purpose was to transmit from teacher to pupil the facts of religion (content-centered) or whether the purpose was to affect lives for good, to change lives toward Christ, with each pupil receiving the personal attention his needs required (life-centered). Along the way, however, the idea emerged that a much better approach would be to combine both. A Christ-centered approach can combine both.

In many of our church schools there are teachers who are aiming at the wrong targets. It is the job of those who guide the school to help them.

Grouping

Although it also has bearing on organization, the placing of a person in the group which gives him the best opportunity is likewise a teaching procedure. Hence, it merits consideration here. Necessarily the consideration will be brief.

The more or less natural tendency of human beings to group them-selves socially by ages has probably influenced teaching procedures from the early days of primitive man. But not very much. The early days of Sunday school in America saw the whole family, from grandparents to lap sitters, seated in the same pew being "taught" the same lesson. The idea of grades—groups made up of persons of approximately the same maturity level—came gradually in Christian education. But ultimately it became securely established as the graded principle dominated public education.

Then, under certain circumstances the pendulum was allowed to swing back a bit. It was recognized that favorable learning situations could be found in groups that cut across age lines. The family, with us all the time but overlooked as a guide to grouping, was suddenly found to be a favorable unit for learning certain things—attitudes, appreciations, and emotional responses mostly, rather than wide ranges of facts. Skill groups often include children and their grandparents with complete congruity.

So we hold to the principle of grading by ages and mental maturity, but at the same time cut squarely across age lines for parts of our church school program. Typically, Sunday school follows a graded pattern, the closeness of the grading usually being directed by the number of persons and the space available. Sunday evening fellowship sees these formal patterns observed for some elements of the program, and completely abandoned for others. And, of course, during-the-week activities have a variety of patterns. Grouping, or not grouping, is determined by the nature of the activity.

All this is important general knowledge for those who guide a church school. An over-all perspective is quite as important as the detailed information possessed by the age-group specialist. And the general administrator must have an over-all perspective.

Methods

An understanding of factors in a long struggle and an insight into the practical are good equipment as one, searching for what is best for today, works his way through the array of teaching methods used by Christian educators now and in the past. New terms do not always mean that what they identify is new. And new developments are to be found clustering around well-worn procedures. The field of method is as exciting as can be found in the educational world today. Extended discussion cannot be undertaken here. Our purpose will be served by bringing into focus common current procedures for brief identification and for comment on the purposes they can serve.

It may be helpful to consider certain principles which apply in the field of method.

There is a relationship between purpose and method. While our great ultimate purpose is stable, our immediate purposes in the operation of a church school are not usually the same for all groups at any given time or for any given group all of the time. Thus the utilization in a church school of a variety of methods may not be evidence of confusion and poor administration. It may be evidence of superior understanding of how learning takes place. This will be discussed further as we proceed.

This fact brings us to the conclusion that flexibility in method should characterize procedures in a group as the immediate purposes of the curriculum vary. It is often desirable that different methods be used in a given group from session to session.

With the desirability of freedom to change methods thus suggested, the next question relates to the exercising of that freedom. Who does the choosing? It is considered good education to give to persons mature and informed enough to have ability to judge freedom to select the method by which they are to be taught. Decision as to where responsibility for choice rests, as between an informed and experienced administrator and an uninformed and inexperienced group, can be a difficult one.

But at stake may be another principle of first magnitude, the principle that method and choice of method contribute to the involvement and the active participation of the learner. A measuring stick by which to evaluate method is the degree of involvement and participation it insures.

Concluding this brief look at some of the principles which should guide in choice of method, is the observation that resident in the method, or among the methods, employed for a given group should be factors which give opportunity for individuals to express and to witness to their growing faith. Valid learnings issue in something. Method should take this into account and provide for outcomes, subjective or objective as normal to the matter under consideration.

We turn now to specific consideration of various methods.

The lecture method is the most condemned and most widely used of any teaching procedure in operation for youth and adults—and unfortunately, often for children. As the word spread that "teaching is more than telling," the idea of a person standing up before a group of other persons and "telling them"—that is, lecturing to them—became increasingly suspect among the informed. It provides practically no opportunity for objective participation and involvement. At its best it can stimulate Christian action, but by no means insures it.

One place where we get into trouble with the lecture method is with the adult class which prefers a procedure that requires least of the members of the class. Many who attend demonstrate that the procedure requires nothing except to be there in body. The lecturer hopes, of course, to command attention. The realization of that hope depends upon his skill. But the number of lives changed toward Christ and vital Christian living by straight lecture is highly conjectural, unless the lecturer-teacher goes into competition with the preacher and delivers a sermon. Though

86

the lecture method is commonly associated with the large, independent adult class which becomes a little church of itself, it is also used widely in other situations.

But to discard the lecture method entirely is probably unwise. Many Christian educators feel that the lecture method is usable providing its use is limited to what it is good for. Since the life of the teacher can teach more than his words, many a lecturer-teacher, himself so close to the Master that the relationship shows through, has led his class into discipleship and has sustained them in the knowledge and the love of Christ despite the handicap of his method. Telling *can* be teaching. Where equipment and teaching skills fall short of being ideal, the lecture can be used for imparting information on straight factual material and for inducing a certain amount of concern for vital Christianity.

Turning from straight lecture, we begin to get on better educational grounds when an opportunity for response by individuals in the group is combined with the lecture. This is an old and often successful method to which new insights give support. The teacher or leader makes his statement (lecture) but reserves sufficient time for (*a*) questions, (*b*) counterstatement, and (*c*) discussion. And, ideally, the teacher-pupil relationship does not end when the class period ends.

Next, very popular and very misused, is the discussion method. It can be highly effective. It can also be disappointingly ineffectual. Yet those who guide the church school do well to make liberal provision for youth and adult groups where the basic procedure is discussion. Discussion is usually integrated into our procedures with children. The discussion method presupposes leaders who have the needed skill and who understand the circumstances under which discussion can be a favorable method. Discussion falls short that does not involve a large portion of the membership. And mere exchange of opinion by uninformed participants may be interesting but may not lead to progress in the Christian life. Yet well-led discussion which insures participation, with sufficient infusion of new factual material and with inspirational stimulation, ranks high as educationally acceptable procedure. It is a highly desirable method among persons willing to think and to submit to the disciplines necessary in a group of participants where growth through interaction of ideas is desired. It is unsuited as a method for promulgation of factual data.

There are many variations. Panel discussions, panel presentations followed by discussion; stories, drama, films, followed by discussion—all have merit.

Team or group teaching is increasingly encountered, particularly (but not exclusively) with children. In true team teaching the usual two to four teachers constitute a true team, all participating actively though seldom simultaneously (unless the group divides into subgroups part of the period). This typically involves a wide range of activities: storytelling, music, reading (research), worship, drama, films and slides, objective materials, spontaneous response, and of course continued participation and leadership on the part of the pupils. The wide popularity of this method is significant for church-school administrators.

Helpful and often startling data have become current in the field of the group process in learning. National leaders in adult work long ago called attention to the fact that a class of adults can reasonably be expected to provide its own teachers from among its own membership. The group process gives us the same assurance, and goes beyond it. Leadership becomes a function of the group itself. To achieve the results that are possible, ways of handling the group procedure from within the group itself must be understood. But those administering a church school today can ill afford to overlook the practical possibilities in this new teaching procedure, which in many respects is not at all new.

Then there are audio-visuals. So much has been written and said about the place of this procedure in the educational program of a church school that it would seem to be a reasonable assumption that by now everyone understands audio-visuals. But actually the assumption is not valid. They are not primarily for entertainment; they are resources for teaching, if skillfully executed they can themselves be teachers, and so on. Observation in many churches forces the conclusion that those who guide a church school should assume the burden of learning to understand the values and the limitations of this increasingly popular and available medium. Wonderfully fine when intelligently used. Less than justifiable when not.

This section should not be concluded without attention being called to the indirect learnings going on all the time. The building teaches, the attitude of the church leaders teaches, the friendliness or indifference of the group teaches. Indeed, a strong case can be made for the point of view that the indirect learnings have more to do with the development of the pupil, one way or the other, than do the direct and planned learnings.

All of this adds up. In a book of this kind extensive descriptions of factors are not possible. Actually, comparatively little can be included in the way of insights into the technical skills so desirable in teachers and leaders. But the conviction does register strongly that church-school administrators must understand that different ways of teaching do exist, that encouragement of their intelligent use should characterize the school, and that teachers who show no inclination or ability to be intelligent in their use of them can hardly be called efficient in this modern world.

How is this to be done? Part of the answer will be found in an alert committee on lesson materials and teaching procedures in your commission on education. Several approaches to leadership education are outlined in denominational literature designed for the guidance of this group.

Program

By program we mean what the church school does.

In some church schools the following of the regular lesson materials provides most of what constitutes their program. They follow this printed material and do, or try to do, what it says and that is that. Actually, they could do far worse. The total curriculum embodied in good lesson materials provides a splendid range of accomplishment that could constitute a really worthwhile program. Such accomplishment is within reach if those who lead have prepared themselves to recognize and take advantage of the ideas the printed curriculum affords.

But there is the possibility of planning and carrying out many vitally important additional things. Most church schools do have activities of one sort and another in addition to those carried in the lesson materials. The special days in the church and community calendar are a constant reminder—Christmas, Easter, Thanksgiving.

Yet all this is not the sum of what an alert church school can do. The commission on education, under imaginative and energetic leadership, can invade the exciting field of tailoring a program to fit the particular needs of the community and even of the individuals the school is reaching. Here is a list of elements into which such a program can be classified. These are referred to again in the chapter on organization.

Winning pupils to Christ and the church
Recruiting and training leaders
Lesson materials and teaching procedures
Increasing membership and attendance
Christian stewardship and giving
Missionary education
Music in Christian education
Christian service and social concerns
Christian family life
Fellowship and recreation
Christian higher education
Organizing and sponsoring outpost church schools.

89

Some of the above relate to program content and some to procedure. Some are relatively constant concerns of the ongoing curriculum and others much less so. But all can contribute to the development, in a given community, of a church-school program appropriate to that community. The commission on education should be encouraged to develop its own list of elements that will compose its program, changing from time to time, and never attempting more or less than the school can reasonably do.

6

ADMINISTRATION AND WORKERS' MEETINGS

Administration

Observations About Administration

The best way to understand good administration is to see it in action. It comes alive as it functions. Good administration is the ingredient that makes our democratically developed plans work. It is the guiding hand engaged in guiding, its skill being measured by the degree to which it not only is unobtrusive, but finally is hardly needed. Good administrators make their services less and less necessary as those with whom they work become more and more able.

Yet administration is not something that ultimately works itself out of a job and is to be discarded.

If administration is conceived as a chain of command, it can be vivid indeed. It can be identified, analyzed, and described. But one would be hard pressed to find anything like a chain of command in our best church schools these days. Instead one finds persons at work, learning and practicing the will of the Lord. Leaders are involved, of course, but not in the sense of "You listen while I tell you." One of the hardest tests administration faces is to succeed at setting up situations which cause persons to understand and to grow. Paul pled with his Galatians to understand and to grow. But they preferred law rather than faith. They wanted a chain of command.

To some it is confusing to be told that a smooth-running organization serving quiet, contented persons is not our goal. They feel that administration is for precisely that. But persons do not *necessarily* either understand or grow just because everything is running smoothly. In a very poor school the machinery could be operating perfectly.

To understand good administration in a church school one must understand good Christian education as it goes on in a good church school. Thus it can be said that helps for understanding administration are diffused throughout this whole book.

Who Administrators Are

The marshalling of the resources of a church school does not come about automatically. The focusing of spiritual power to overcome evil does not just happen. And the establishing and the reaching of courageous goals do not transpire without guidance. The nature of guidance determines the appropriateness of administrative techniques in Christian education. And all this leads to the question, "Who are the administrators in a church school?"

One answer is, the general officers. General officers are those who serve the school as a whole, as contrasted with those who serve only a segment, that is, church-school superintendent, assistant superintendents, membership cultivation superintendent, general secretary, general treasurer, and perhaps librarian and literature secretary. Some would include among the general officers the director of Christian education, the pastor, and the chairman of the commission on education, though the chairman is not actually in the administrative group.

But others are administrators also. Division and department heads certainly are administrators. In a sense, all church-school officers are administrators.

92

Administrative Relationships

The pastor has ultimate responsibility for the church school in the sense that he has responsibility for the whole local church. But the wise pastor works through his laymen to the greatest extent possible. His role is that of spiritual guide, wise counselor, educator of leaders, sometimes teacher, and always inspirer and encourager.

The director of Christian education often is forced out of his normal role. Circumstances may cause him to take administrative responsibility, sometimes even assuming specific administrative jobs such as securing teachers. But where this occurs, the director is functioning at less than his highest level of efficiency. Basically, the director is an experienced, professionally trained person who helps the leaders in the church school do the best possible job. As in the case of the pastor, the director is an advisor and an encourager, but typically majors in training leadership. The church-school superintendent, not the director, is the administrative head of the church school.

The chairman of the commission on education is a presiding officer, not an executive or administrative person. He heads the "legislative branch" (policy making) of the work.

The church-school superintendent heads the "executive branch" of the work, leading those who carry out the policies made by the commission on education (the "legislative branch"). He is, however, a member of the commission on education and thus is involved in policy making.

The membership cultivation superintendent, the general secretary, treasurer, and the other general officers work under the general administrative direction of the church-school superintendent, within the policies of the commission.

The division and department superintendents are assistants to the church-school superintendent within their own fields of work, administering their part of the school under his general direction. And the teachers and other workers are administratively under the department and division superintendents.

But this matter of administrative relationships must not be left with just this statement. The way in which the administrator proceeds is the vital element in success. It must be abundantly clear that in a church school the administrator deals with those administratively "under" him, not as one who commands but rather as one who suggests and advises. "He who would be greatest among you must be servant of all." This is true not only because it is the Christian approach to the operation of the church, but also because we have no "career" administrators in a well-conducted church school. Rotation in office and limited tenure, as well as limited knowledge on the part of many who hold office, suggest the ineptness of administration being thought of as a chain of command.

This brings us logically to the next topic.

Supervision

Reactions to the idea of supervision in an average church school will vary. Here are three different but familiar ones: (a) Fine. Let's have it. (b) No! We don't want any snoopervision around here. (c) Probably all right, but we don't know enough. The officers are no wiser than the teachers. The trainer must know more than the dog. Better forget about it.

But judgment and decision about supervision should involve an understanding of what it is. What is supervision in a church school?

A dictionary definition will be of little help. Actually in educational circles, both church and secular, the idea is in flux. Not only are ideas about supervision changing, but not all proposed changes are acceptable to all educators.

At the risk of oversimplification, some answers can be given.

Where imparting religious facts, rather than guiding persons in Christian development, is the objective the supervisor may be thought of as an overseer who directs the teachers in following the routines calculated to fix facts in pupils' minds. This could be a chain of command affair. That is not necessarily repugnant to the individual oriented toward imparting information rather than toward the dignity of persons in process of developing Christlikeness.

But where the Christian development of persons is the direct objective, supervision can hardly be like that. With the supervisor respecting the pupil as a developing Christian, it is natural that the teacher should likewise be respected. Presently all are learners together—pupil, teacher, and supervisor. The teacher tries to set up situations in which the pupil will change through personal involvement. Likewise the supervisor tries to set up situations in which the teacher will change through personal involvement.

In the first instance, above, supervision is inspection and judgment. In the second, it is wise helpfulness. Theory governing supervision is determined by theory governing education. Fortunately, within reach of many local churches are interested public school personnel who are skilled in supervision and willing to help us understand its application in church school.

If supervision is to be undertaken, who in the average church school will serve as supervisors? In small schools, the superintendent. In larger schools, the division superintendent; if departmentalized, the department superintendent. In team teaching the lead teacher can be a supervisor, or the responsibility can rotate within the team. Then how would one proceed as a supervisor?

Suppose an old-fashioned deportment problem is to be faced. Try this: In workers' conference have a panel followed by discussion. The panel might include (a) an older junior high, (b) a parent of a junior high, (c) a teacher of junior highs, (d) a public-school teacher or supervisor who knows good public-school education for this age. The public-school teacher could serve as panel leader and feed in facts about deportment problems for this age, including causes as well as solutions.

This is one way to carry on supervision. But suppose some kindly teacher, in a fog about the whole matter, comes to a department superintendent for help. There is nothing to prevent an able superintendent from giving help right then and there. And good supervision includes, under favorable circumstances, a superintendent initiating conversations with teachers concerning their work. That, too, is supervision. Its quality, of course, depends upon the ideas the superintendent has. No one method of supervision commands the approval of all educators.

Consider these suggestions for the deportment problem:

1. Poor deportment can be a symptom of some deeper ill. Or, it can be a transitory humor that flits across the surface of a perfectly wonderful class.

2. If it is a symptom of a deeper ill, begin the search for the cause by taking a look at the way the teacher teaches.

a) Is the teacher's point of view "I am teaching lessons," or is it "I am trying to guide persons"?

b) Is the teacher "inside the group" or "outside the group"? That is, does the teacher enter, in ways possible to an adult, into the world of the age being taught? Are there social contacts, during-the-week contacts in recreation or in other ways, interesting to the class? Does the teacher limit his job to the time the class is in session? Has the teacher really been accepted by the class?

c) Does the teacher do a good or a poor job of lesson preparation using the teaching helps and entering into the spirit of the lesson as planned by the lesson writers?

3. Are there observable abnormalities about the ring leaders in deportment outbursts? Are they problem persons? If so, consultation with parents and competent counselors may prove wise.

The reader, having read this brief section on supervision, might well conclude: "You call this supervision? I'd call it plain old training. All this belongs over in the chapter on leadership." Perhaps it does. The trend in supervision is certainly in the direction of helping workers improve their understandings and their skills.

Workers' Meetings

Akin to administration is the planning of the work that is to be administered. Therefore, this chapter includes both administration and workers' meetings. The workers' meetings to be discussed are the commission on education, the workers' conference, the division and department councils, and the meetings of teaching teams. What is the purpose of each? How can they be made to succeed?

Basic to an understanding of what to do to make workers' meetings "succeed" is comprehension of principles governing how leadership is effectively exerted. A simple question serves to introduce the matter: "Why do we have workers' meetings?" A full answer requires complicated analyses, but there is a direct answer which covers most of the ground. It is, "To provide a working fellowship where minds and hearts can meet creatively and together reach decisions, achieve understandings, gain insights, acquire skills, upon which effective progress depends."

Stated another way, a brilliant leader working alone will fail where a group of normally capable persons working and praying together will succeed. This applies to planning and policy making rather than to administration, of course.

This is not universally understood. Some administrators do not want to be bothered by committees, commissions, and other deliberative groups. They prefer to make the decisions as well as to execute them. Seldom are the schools they "run" truly successful. More often though there is a conscientious effort to have workers' meetings, but without procedures undergirded by right principles they fail.

Unembellished, the principle at the heart of the matter is this: In the fellowship of the followers of Christ, which is the church, planning and working together is the necessary condition for significant progress.

The Commission on Education

Every church school, small or large, needs a deliberative body to do basic planning, establish policy, and exercise basic control. The usual alternative is a superintendent who carries responsibility for everything. That is a poor alternative.

Typical among Protestant denominations, The Methodist Church makes this provision:

In order that a local church may be so organized and administered as to provide effectively for the Christian education of its entire constituency, there shall be a Commission on Education in each local church. It shall be auxiliary to the Annual Conference and Jurisdictional Boards of Education and to the Division of the Local Church of the General Board of Education.[1]

Here is a condensation of its major functions. It shall:

—Determine policy for the church school and give general direction to all the educational work of the church.
—Study the educational needs of the church; organize and guide the church school.
—Supervise ordering of teaching materials, including audio-visuals, and insure use of approved materials only.
—Win pupils to Christ and church membership.
—Provide for reaching the constituency through membership and attendance increase and through outpost church schools.
—Insure use of the church-school record system.
—Supervise the selection and use of music in the church school and the integration of children's and youth choirs into the Christian education program for children and youth.
—Insure the enlistment and training of teachers and leaders.
—Plan and supervise the church-school budget.

The membership of the commission on education reflects the theory of Christian education which governs. If teaching is considered a way of communicating the gospel in its full richness, just as are preaching and witnessing, then the church school will include in the scope of its endeavor all the basic elements that make up the program of the church, that is, evangelism, missions, stewardship, Christian social concerns, and the like. And if the church school is to function in all these areas, then its governing body (the commission on education) should include in its membership, representatives from the other commissions which carry these particular responsibilities. In addition, of course, would be representatives from the congregation at large, including parents and older youth. The various organizations of the church (woman's society, men's organization, and the like) would have representation. And of course the general officers and division superintendents are included.

[1] *Discipline,* op. cit., ¶ 231.

It is not considered good practice for the church-school superintendent to serve as chairman of the commission on education. It is important to distinguish between the legislative and the administrative functions. The chairman heads the legislative (policy making and basic planning) operations, and the superintendent the administrative. Experience in civil government and in the church school indicates the inadvisability of lodging these two responsibilities in the same person. There is also the very practical consideration that each is a big job in itself and both can hardly be handled well by one person.

The commission on education can proceed without any organization except president and secretary, or it can organize itself elaborately. Typically, the program areas listed on p. 89 should have committees or designated persons to insure adequate consideration.

In a successful church school, meetings of the commission at least monthly will be required. Always there should be an agenda made up in advance by the chairman in consultation with the church-school superintendent, the pastor, and the director of Christian education, where there is one. In the course of a year all of the program areas felt to be important in your church school (see the thirteen suggested on p. 89) should have a place on the agenda.

Is "beginning and closing meetings on schedule" such a hackneyed statement as not to merit room on this page? Perhaps, but a successful chairman takes that statement seriously. The same can be said for: (a) unfailing courtesy, (b) enough parliamentary procedure to make the meeting orderly, but not so much as to be stilted or get in the way of easy informality, (c) respect for opinions of all (here can function the Christian concept of the blessed community where effort is made to understand and support each other and together accomplish what cannot be done separately), (d) such skillful chairmanship as prevents monopoly of time by any, (e) a constant eye on the agenda and the clock to insure transaction of necessary business. This list could be continued. Well-conducted meetings find reflection in church-school progress.

One additional item: Adequate records are essential. The secretary who keeps the minutes should be given specific guidance as to the way the body wants its minutes kept. The physical form of minutes should be prescribed—loose-leaf typed, or longhand in a bound book, or mimeographed and distributed. Determine custody of minutes and where the permanent record should be kept year after year. Future chairmen will bless the thoughtful persons who give attention to these details.

The Workers' Conference

What has been said in the above section about agenda, conduct of meetings, skills of chairman, minutes, and the like, applies to the workers' conference, of course. While it is highly questionable for the church-school superintendent to serve as chairman of the commission, it is definitely wise for him to be chairman of the workers' conference. The agenda for meetings is his responsibility, but invariable consultation with the other leaders in its development is important. Some workers' conferences have an agenda committee, of which the church-school superintendent is chairman.

But what, specifically, is the purpose of the workers' conference? How does it differ from the commission on education? Who composes it? How often should it meet? In the very small church, are both necessary or even possible? Answers to these and other questions will be suggested. There are certain generally accepted approaches. But each church school must decide many of these things for itself. The membership of the workers' conference, though, is rather universally agreed upon. It is composed of *all* officers, teachers, and workers. If there is any doubt as to whether a person is a member, give him the benefit of the doubt and include him.

In the preceding section the purpose of the commission on education is suggested as being the deliberative body needed to do basic planning, establish policy, and exercise basic control over the church school. In sharp contrast to that, it is suggested that the purpose of the workers' conference be: (*a*) Christian fellowship, (*b*) study, (*c*) discussion. On the surface, if these three things constitute the purpose of a workers' conference, its importance to the church school might be questioned. But careful consideration will reveal that in these three items we actually have tremendous assets that can bear directly on the success of a church school.

Consider Christian fellowship. In itself it is enjoyable. But the chief reason for desiring it for our teachers and workers is what it makes possible. If throughout the school teachers and workers are happy, friendly, loyal, and enthusiastic, that school is well on its way to success. If the reverse is true, the technical skills they may possess will count for little. Morale is just that important. It follows, then, that the church-school superintendent, and all who share with him responsibility for the workers' conference will do well to give major attention to making every session yield as much as possible in the way of Christian fellowship.

How? Two suggestions: (*a*) Put your own wits to work on the matter and come up with some good ideas. (b) Consider these morale boosters:

—Go all out for hospitality. Friendly greeters at the door. The church-school superintendent and the three division superintendents circulating through the group (before time to begin the meeting) engaging early arrivals in conversation that evidences personal interest.
—Give special attention to new members of the group, presenting them in the meeting and making them welcome.
—Take note of interesting things that relate to members of the group, such as family events (new babies, successes in school, birthdays and other anniversaries, any sort of good news).
—Emphasize what is encouraging and set the tone for optimism.
—Involve the membership in being hospitable and friendly to each other.
—Interpret Christian work as a joyous thing.

Consider next the second purpose for workers' conference—study. How could anything be less attractive? Who wants to study? But if we will interpret this purpose broadly to mean increasing the skills of teachers and workers, the idea holds great possibilities. And here open up for us the ways in which the workers' conference can provide opportunities to further the training of teachers and workers. In the chapter on leaders this is discussed, but a few examples can be listed here:

—Brief reviews of training texts to stimulate personal reading
—Fifteen-minute presentations of chapters from books relating to the work
—Panel discussions on practical aspects of teaching and of lesson preparation
—Talks by persons skilled in education (public-school people often are available)
—Distribution for quick reading of clippings from the church-school magazines and other publications
—Films and filmstrips. There are tremendous possibilities here.

The third suggested purpose for the workers' conference is discussion. By that is meant discussion of the work of the church school, in order that all may be informed of plans and policies developed in the commission on education and in order that suggestions to pass on to the commission may emerge. In church schools large enough to have division and department councils, much of this function can be referred to them, leaving for discussion in the workers' conference only those matters of general concern. Thus, the workers' conference provides a way to implement the policy decisions and the general planning done in the commission on education.

How often should the workers' conference meet? Again, that depends on the local situation, the frequence of other workers' meetings being a factor. But with the commission on education meeting monthly, it is considered good practice for the workers' conference to meet quarterly.

We still have before us for consideration the problem of the very small church where, it seems, the same people are unavoidably involved in everything. Specifically, is it practical under such circumstances to try to have both a commission on education and a workers' conference? Often the answer must be no. Yet, a word of caution is appropriate. Combining the two should be occasioned by necessity, not convenience.

Using the combination presents some questions. What shall the group be called? Who shall be chairman? What functions are assigned? Since normally the commission on education elects the teachers, how avoid the awkward situation of teachers being members of the body which elects them? Here are the suggested answers: The combined group is called the commission on education. The person elected as chairman of the commission would serve as chairman rather than the church-school superintendent. However, the superintendent should be given every opportunity to accomplish in the meetings things which he would normally get done in a workers' conference meeting, within the limitations which the combination imposes. The combined group should take over the functions of the two groups in so far as possible. And when time comes to elect teachers, dispense with the combination and let the few who would compose the commission itself do the electing.

Division and Department Councils

Because size and circumstances vary so greatly, only general observations are possible concerning division and department councils. Frankly the workers in a church school face an imposing time schedule when the full list of workers' groups are attempted. Commission on education (monthly), workers' conference (quarterly), division council (monthly —or how often?), department council (monthly—or how often?), plus other church obligations which practically every active person will carry in addition—all these add up to a large total.

Yet so many church schools find a place and a need for this whole list of meetings, and succeed so well in using them all effectively, that any suggestion that some of them could be omitted would be unwise. Often the solution is found by making the department council a more intimate working group, meeting more often than the division council with the division council functioning in the main as an age group committee of the commission on education. This is discussed further in the chapter on organization.

Teaching Teams

Because the work of a teaching team is within the context of the curriculum, its function, procedure, and the meetings needed for preparation all are directly or inferentially prescribed in the curriculum. Hence, no treatment is needed here. Indeed the procedures of a teaching team are so completely conditioned by the immediate job before them, and are so variable from unit to unit, that treatment apart from the context would be impossible, except for generalities. But team teaching has become an established fact. It is employed across the nation in church schools, small and large. So the planning meeting of teaching teams has a place in the consideration of the list of workers' meetings.

Attendance at Workers' Meetings

What question is more frequently asked than "How do you get people to attend meetings?" There often is something hopeless about it as though they had tried everything and did not expect an answer. But there is an answer. Basically, the answer is common sense and hard work.

The competition for people's time these days is fierce, and is apt to get worse rather than better. Like so much else in the Christian program, success demands a heavy investment of self. There are no permanently successful tricks or shortcuts to insuring good attendance at workers' meetings. But there are some guide lines that the good administrator never ignores. Whatever else he may do, these he always includes. Note:

The bedrock foundation for good attendance is to have something worth attending. Christian loyalty on the part of the workers cannot reasonably be expected to bring them to a meeting that offers little promise of advancing the Christian cause, particularly if they have come in the past and have found nothing. Take this seriously. Here is the place to begin solving the problem of poor attendance at workers' meetings. Publicity and enthusiasm cannot be honest if the meeting itself lacks quality. Bring to bear on the program planning and preparation for a meeting all the insights and understandings at your command. Insure a good program at the meeting by paying the price necessary to have it.

Does your leadership training program include elements that will result in understanding the whole responsibility of a worker? A teacher may attend courses that will help him know the Bible, without it ever occurring to him that attending workers' meetings is also part of the teachers' business.

Around your church is Christianity interpreted as discipleship? And is it clear that a disciple *works* for his Master? And is attendance at

102

workers' meetings clearly understood as an obligation as well as an opportunity? In your church school is it your regular practice to discuss with each new teacher and worker what his responsibilities will be, including the fact that attendance at workers' meetings is not optional, but necessary?

In other words, do your teachers and workers think of attendance at workers' meeting as being on the same level of importance as teaching the class or otherwise discharging their immediate responsibilities? Make attention to this business a normal part of the workers' duties.

Then, of course, there is the matter of publicity. This includes both information and reminders. On paper make a list of all that you do to insure good attendance at workers' meetings. Can you improve your own list? Do you have a regular schedule for your meetings so that the time can be reserved in the workers' personal calendars? Do all understand clearly when and where the meetings are to be held? And do you remind them? Do notices go out by mail? Is every member phoned during the day for an evening meeting?

The above are standard things that good church-school administrators know and do, regardless of what they may do in addition. But what could they do in addition?

The administrator who is so in earnest about the workers' meetings for which he is responsible, that his prayers and his central interests are invested, will find that his earnestness is contagious. This is a test of the genuineness of the administrator. But can he go even further? He wants the workers to come. Is he willing also to go to them? The leader who visits purposefully in the homes of his workers will usually find that they will respond and come to workers' meetings.

Common sense procedures and hard work along experience-tested guide lines will improve attendance at workers' meetings. If you can add to these your own prayer-guided personal touches, you are not apt to be among those who ask "How can you get people to come to workers' meetings?"

7

ROLLS, RECORDS, REPORTS, EVALUATION

Those who guide a church school, and likewise those who work with the smallest class in it, can be helped greatly by trustworthy information about what actually is going on. The attitude is occasionally encountered that record keeping is unimportant and even out of place in a spiritual enterprise. That, of course, is a false notion. It is true that undue emphasis on records can absorb energies needed otherwise. But properly devised and appropriately used rolls, records, and reports are vital necessities in a well-conducted church school.

Akin to the need for information which records can reveal is the need for being in position to take stock of where we are—to evaluate. Those who guide a church school face the necessity of interpreting the information gained from records and reports if they are to proceed wisely. Those who guide the Christian development of individual pupils likewise are helped if they have ways to measure progress.

This is the field of this chapter.

Church School Membership

Before there can be a sound basis for records and reports, there must be an understanding of what a church school is and of what constitutes membership in it. In Chap. IX the nature of the modern church school is discussed. Described there are the basic parts suggested for a complete church school as it has emerged to meet today's needs, that is, (a) the Sunday morning session of classes and groups conventionally referred to as Sunday school, (b) the Sunday evening fellowship groups, (c) week-day activities, and (d) the home and extension services. Naturally, one becomes a member of the church school when he becomes a member in any of these parts.

Likewise a moment's attention can profitably be given to terminology. Which term is preferable, "enrollment" or "membership"? Long habit causes some to refer to "church membership" and "church-school enrollment." But it is suggested that the term "enrollment" is inadequate for the modern approach to Christian education. The term "membership" is more appropriate. The difference is not in the basic meaning of the two terms. The difference is in the inferences which have grown up around them.

The term "enrollment" has come to be associated with limited term enterprises. One refers to the enrollment for the fall quarter in the freshman class at college. But a person's relationship to church school is different. It should be permanent. Hence the wisdom of avoiding the use of a term associated with impermanence. Membership seems more suitable because it does not wear a tag.

What is involved here is not a quibbling over terms. The deeper consideration here is the long struggle to make Christian education a permanent, continuing experience. For too long too many persons have thought of relationship to church school as seasonal and often limited to childhood.

This matter has bearing on rolls and record keeping. In the days when Sunday school got under way in the early fall (after the summer vacation or the summer "slump") and then disbanded in the late spring, enrollment was a proper term. The enterprise was on a term basis. Often the rolls were thrown away in the spring. A new start was made each fall when operations began again, and the enrollment was built up throughout the season. No names were dropped until the whole list was discarded at the end of the term. Enrollment meant the total number of names put on the roll during the year regardless of dropouts. There were many variations, of course.

But a different point of view now obtains concerning the Christian educational work of the church. Christian education is now thought of as a continuing ministry of the church to persons of all ages under all circumstances. The emphasis has shifted from a term relationship which kept track of the total number involved during a period of time, to a continuing personal relationship. Instead of being enrolled for a course, one becomes a permanent member of a continuing enterprise. (Do not be confused by short curriculum units or realignment of classes from time to time. That can take place within the permanent, continuing membership in the church school.) We work toward the concept of membership in the teaching ministry of the church. Hence the use of *membership* instead of *enrollment*. And hence, also, the permanence of our membership rolls.

It is truly said that the time to become a member of the church school is the day you are born (nursery home roll) and the time to terminate that membership is the day you die. Our focus is on the fact that church-school membership should be valued by the individual and the church school and protected in the record system, just as membership in the church itself is protected.

The Rolls

The secretarial work in all church schools, small and large, is made up of three elements: (*a*) the rolls (the membership rolls of individual names), (*b*) the records (attendance, offering, and the like), and (*c*) the reports. As in other major denominations, The Methodist Church publishes its own system, known as the Methodist Church-School Record System. It is designed to meet the special needs of the church schools of the denomination.

We begin our consideration with the rolls.

An accurate roll of members is the foundation of the church school's records. Keeping that roll is a service of dignity and worth to the Kingdom and an important element in our effort to help immortal souls grow toward Christ.

Every church school, except perhaps the very smallest, should have two kinds of rolls, as follows:

1. *The working roll.* This is the membership roll kept by each class or

106

group. The teachers and leaders work with it continually, checking attendance and the like. Most schools have this working roll in one form or another.

2. *The central roll.* In addition to the working rolls the general secretary should have a central roll on which are kept the names and necessary information concerning every person who appears on any of the working rolls, that is, of every member of the church school.

The reason for the central roll is to provide a way (*a*) to know how many members the church school has, (*b*) to know who the members are, (*c*) to have at hand helpful information about all of them, and (*d*) to protect church-school membership from the hazards of careless handling by the many persons who use the working rolls of classes and groups. Church-school membership is not a matter of lumping together all the working rolls of classes and groups. The reason it is not, is that a person may, and frequently does, belong to more than one group in the church school, and merely putting the working rolls together would involve counting a person more than once. In the central roll, kept alphabetically, a person's name appears only once regardless of the number of groups in the church school in which he has membership.

With each name on the central roll there is opportunity to list data concerning the person. At a glance, his relationships to church-school and church activities can be revealed, such as whether or not a member of the church. The evangelistic work of the church school is greatly aided by a well-kept central roll.

In the church-school record system referred to above, the working rolls can be kept on loose cards, in small class books, or on punched cards in visual ring binders. In this system the central roll can be kept on loose cards in a card file or on punched cards in visual ring binders.

The Records

The rolls provide the names and personal information concerning the membership. The records provide information on such progress items as attendance, offering, expenditures, and growth in membership, collected in one general record book in the custody of the general secretary. At each level of organization (class or group, department, division, and school as a whole) the responsible officials have the duty of keeping informed concerning detailed developments in the area of their responsibility. This is what records are for. Unfortunately, there are teachers and officers who do not understand this and the records, which stand ready to guide them, sometimes receive scant attention.

The Reports

Filling out report forms is for many an unpleasant duty. Perhaps this is occasioned by lack of information as to the value of good reports. Or it could be that their information is all too accurate about the way reports are lightly held by those receiving them. In any event those charged with guiding a church school will do well to give mature consideration to this part of their responsibility. The saying that "knowledge is power" can apply here.

To what use can reports be put?

Consider the annual reports of the church school as a whole which finally find their way, along with other data from the local church, into the over-all statistics of the denomination. If individually these reports are accurate, the denominational statistics are trustworthy and national policy and program can be intelligently devised. Thus the progress of the Christian church as the Body of Christ, working for the salvation of mankind, is involved. Faithful attention to supplying data at the source assumes importance and dignity.

But within the local church and its church school there is very much the same need. How does the official board of the church know, accurately, about the operation of the church school? It can know only from reports—written and oral. Yet how very often such reports are trivial, vague, and boring.

It is even more important that the commission on education have constantly before it complete and trustworthy reports covering every phase of the operation of the church school. A good reporting system provides this. Statistics can readily be conveyed in written reports. But so can overtones and informed impressions, which can so greatly help the commission in its work. Church-school officers should subject themselves to the discipline of making brief, intelligent, written reports.

One illustration of the value to a specific official of trustworthy reports is the dependence of the membership cultivation superintendent upon them. The health of a church school is revealed in its reports in that, except in unusual cases, a church school which is not growing is in questionable health. But much more than statistics is involved in good reports, as will be discussed in the following section on measurements.

Evaluation

There can be no quarrel with the idea that the measurement of progress is an important function of those who guide a church school. Intelligent evaluation is an indispensable ingredient in wise planning and

108

administration. But what should be measured and how it can be measured are imposing questions.

Ultimately the church school stands or falls on whether or not individual church-school members are growing toward Christ and devoting themselves to him, are increasing in understanding and practicing Christianity, and are effectively helping to make the gospel real in the lives of others. That is, our question about what should be measured finds its first answer in the individual church-school member. Likewise our greatest difficulty in measuring will be found to center here.

Classes and groups are to be evaluated. This is true regardless of whether they are fixed units in the church-school organization or are fluid and re-formed from time to time. Relationship of size of class to the capacity of the quarters it occupies is a concern. Evaluation must be present here. Growth, or lack of it, is involved. The spirit of the group is a central factor for measurement. Is the group really producing? And what is it producing?

The evaluation spotlight likewise falls upon the teachers, the leaders, the officers. How do they measure up? What are the causes for their brilliant success or their dull mediocrity? Were they wisely chosen? Is the procedure for selecting teachers a sound one? Or, are failures in the provision for training and helping teachers grow, showing up as the real deterrents to progress? The evaluation of leaders is part of the picture.

And there must be measurement of the church school as a whole. This is going on continually in informal and incidental ways. But there is need for critical evaluation from time to time on as thorough a basis as possible. There must be constant evaluation of the effect the church school has in terms of the goals and purposes of the local church itself. How adequately does the church school contribute to those goals and purposes?

But our measurements must reach out beyond our organization and our within-the-walls program. What results, if any, can be found in the families connected with our church school and in the new families founded by those who grow up in our care? And what about our impact on the community? Does our being here make any real difference in the social structure in which the church school has its setting?

Actually, our concern for evaluation and the factors we undertake to measure will be dictated by our philosophy of Christian education. If, basically, we operate on the level of transmitting information only, our excursions into the realm of measurements will be limited to mechanical tests of knowledge. This is relatively easy. But if, basically, we operate on the level of life transformation with our goals the highest in Christian conception, our attempts at measurement will reflect that fact. And measurement here is desperately hard, so hard that many hold it to be impossible.

Anything like complete and satisfactory handling of this matter of evaluation would include descriptions of instruments and procedures for each of the fields of our concern, from the individual church-school member to our impact on the local community and even, in a limited sense, the world beyond. Since completely acceptable instruments and procedures do not exist, we must settle for less than our ideal as we discuss evaluation in the church school. Through the years in which Christian education has had a place in the work and the structure of the church, no one thing has more often called the best leadership together for another try in the face of previous failures, than the search for a break-through in effective measurement in Christian education.

Some attractive procedures and even instruments do exist and reference will be made to them later in this section. And some rather popular approaches can be faced and, frankly, be ruled out. For instance, some "Standards of Efficiency for Church Schools." Most of the lists of "ten points" (more or less), often including provision to score the church school on its degree of excellence, promise more than they deliver. They can help rally the forces of the church school, work up enthusiasm and loyalty, and perhaps finally belong on the plus side in the life of the church school. But as real measures of spiritual factors they are hard to defend.

Some of these "standards," though, have value if their limitations are understood. They cannot measure the individual spiritual progress of members, but they can point the way to what is considered good program development and good organization and administration procedures. The *Check List of Responsibilities of the Commission on Education,* issued by The Methodist Church, is an illustration. Within its field it is helpful. It does provide an instrument by which to evaluate the procedures of a commission on education. It is a 24-page booklet. It contains 109 evaluation questions which are to be checked poor, fair, or good. These are grouped under thirteen topics ranging from success at winning pupils to Christ and church membership to organizing and sponsoring outpost church schools. It is synchronized with the denomination's *Manual for the Commission on Education.* It does indeed serve as a check list on the extent to which a local church school is at work in the various fields suggested as making up the program of an effective church school. But, of course, it does not measure results in Christian living.

Here is still another approach to the evaluation of a church school: From a practical standpoint those who guide a church school need to know two things, (a) are the procedures being used in the church school the best that we know, and (b) are the results being achieved in the lives of members and in the relationships of the church school measuring up to what is desired? The following listing suggests ways of getting at answers to these two questions:

1. Helpful procedures

Certain procedures will aid in achieving desired results. A school is proceeding effectively if it incorporates the following in an intelligent and adequate degree:

—adequate program
—proper literature and materials
—good teaching methods
—appropriate organization
—adequate leadership
—provision for increase and expansion
—adequate housing and equipment
—home and church-school co-operation

2. Desired results

The effectiveness of a church school can be measured only by the results it is getting. If the answer to these questions is yes, and in satisfactory measure, the results are effective.

—Are you helping people know God through Christ?
—Are you winning people to Christ and church membership?
—Are you producing persons for church vocations?
—Are you achieving Christian use of money?
—Are you growing in church-school membership and attendance?
—Are you establishing outposts where needed?
—Are you developing service habits and helping community betterment?
—Are you establishing habits of church attendance and participation in the church program?
—Are you developing Christian homes?
—Are you developing habits of worship and use of the Bible?

But the heart of the matter may still not have been touched. The chief thing that needs to be measured in a church school is the spiritual progress of individual members.

For many years researchers have been at work, refusing to settle for objective, mechanical measurements, such as, "Brought Bible," "Perfect Attendance," "Contributed an Offering," or even "Volunteered for Christian Service." Again and again the verdict has been "What we are after is imponderable. You can't measure a person's spiritual life."

But the search goes on. A penetrating analysis of the problems involved

111

will be found in *Evaluation and Christian Education,* available from National Council of Churches, 475 Riverside Drive, New York 27, New York.

However, for the average church school, guided by lay persons who quite understandably do not possess professional skills either in education or theology, the matter of how to measure individual spiritual progress, remains an unanswered question.

Except that—practical, godly people, experienced in the things of God and of the world, who have been around church schools for some time, are apt to be able to tell you which teachers are getting good results and which are not. They may possess no measuring instrument and may be unable to converse on the psychological aspects of character development, but they know when a boy or girl is turning out all right. And they know when a man is being redeemed from an evil life. And they know whether their church school is getting somewhere or not.

The point is that those who guide a church school need to evaluate the school and its product, whether this is done through skillful utilization of what is available in technical measurements or through practical observation. It is important to know where you want to go, and how far you have traveled along the way.

8

PROGRAM, BUDGETS, AND FINANCE

What This Chapter Undertakes

Church schools come in all sizes with membership from less than a dozen up to several thousand. There would be endless detail in a full consideration of all their financial aspects, but many helpful suggestions can be made.

Here is a statement of financial policy for a church school: The classes turn their offerings over to the treasurer and he pays the bills.

Few of us, though, would think that a sufficient guide for financial operations, even in a very small church school. But if this is not a sufficient guide for financial operations, what would be? This chapter undertakes to help answer that question. It undertakes also to offer help in relating budget to program.

The commission on education should be responsible for establishing and maintaining policy to govern financial matters throughout the church school. This is in keeping with the commission's comprehensive responsibility for the church school. This sense of responsibility also should guide the commission in keeping church-school financial policy in harmony with the total financial plans of the local church.

A statement of the financial policy of the church school should appear in the records of the commission and should be understood by workers throughout the church school. It should be available to the official board and to the commission on stewardship and finance. A pattern for such a policy statement appears on p. 134.

Spiritual Factors

1. *Stewardship is a spiritual matter.* There are spiritual factors in good financial policy. They are of utmost importance. The financial operations of a church school should be based on the divine call for sharing and sacrifice in the noblest cause known to man. We operate on the principle that God is the owner and man is the trustee. This is not to question the ethics of legal ownership in an earthly sense. It is simply to affirm that the legal owner is accountable to God, the real owner in the ultimate sense. In his relationship to the money he possesses, a Christian is always conscious of his accountability to God.

Stewardship properly understood is an intensely spiritual matter. Stewardship education is a vital part of Christian education and is one of the basic responsibilities of the church school. Church-school curriculum includes stewardship education. Teachers and workers have continuing opportunity to teach the spiritually based concept of Christian stewardship.

2. *Motivation for giving.* As one matures in Christian knowledge, things often need to be unlearned. This sometimes is accomplished by the substitution of a more accurate idea. Among the spiritual factors involved in stewardship are those which deal with motives for giving. Sometimes these motives are less than good and should be replaced by better ones. Illustrations follow:

The Christian teacher frequently encounters giving based on payment for value received or to be received. It's an "I'll pay my way" sort of thing. Shocking though it is, some giving is to buy respectability or some other form of security. "I help pay the preacher's salary. In return I expect from him service of various sorts. I help finance missions around the world. As a consequence I expect, frankly, protection in some degree from unfortunate happenings that occur to others." Matters are on a transaction basis. And when unfortunate things do happen to givers who have these motives, they feel they have been dealt with unfairly. They pay and they expect to get value received in one way or another. This is giving, but it is not stewardship. The Christian teacher works to replace such motives with more worthy ones.

Again, the Christian teacher encounters giving occasioned by fear. It is almost a matter of "The goblins will get you if you don't watch out." Perhaps this is a carry-over from the heathen practice of appeasing the gods. This error in motive for giving roots, of course, in one's idea of God. The Christian's God does not have to be appeased. Giving based on fear of consequences if one does not give, may bless the recipient, but leaves the giver with nothing except a temporary respite from his fears.

A much higher motive is giving because of a sense of duty. Many very fine persons operate on this level. It has much to commend it. Probably a sense of duty enters into the stewardship practices of all Christians. Yet, if we are searching for the highest motive, we will not stop here.

Akin to stewardship based on duty is giving because of gratitude. Surely this is worthy. Unmerited blessing has come to us. Out of hearts filled with gratitude we, in turn, give that others may be blessed. But there is something higher still. The Christian teacher who guides others in understanding the spiritual factors involved in stewardship and finance will not stop short of love and compassion as the truly Christian motive for giving.

Compassionate giving is best of all. Here is stewardship in its highest form. One gives because of love for God and love for fellow man. Something in return is not involved. Fear has no part. Duty may be present but it is a minor element. Gratitude there is, of course, because all of us are recipients of God's grace, but compassionate giving continues even when the giver is himself going through the dark valley and there seems little for which to be grateful.

How can the Christian teacher lead others to give their money and themselves because of love? There can be only one answer. When one's life is hidden in the life of the Savior who in compassionate love gave all, then one is in position to exercise his stewardship on that supreme level. It finally develops that the highest in stewardship rests on the highest in evangelism and in Christian nurture.

3. *Importance of highest motivation.* Church-school leaders, general officers as well as teachers, have the opportunity to guide pupils into worthy motives for giving. Indeed, when this has been done, budgets and other items of church-school finance constitute no problem. If a person is truly anchored in a knowledge of God's love and responds with genuine

115

love and compassion for mankind, he will share what he has because of that love.

This has a practical application. Some church schools, and their churches, major in financial campaigns, pressure, and devices of various sorts to "raise the budget." Other church schools and churches major in teaching Christian motives for giving. The latter finds that budgets and finance can be handled with a minimum of difficulty.

The glory of doing the will of God is certainly present here. Our problem is to handle financial matters in such a way that the spiritual aspects govern and that people will give because of a truly Christian motive—a real desire to help in accomplishing God's purposes. The way in which Jesus related godly living to the handling of money is well understood by careful readers of the New Testament. It is revealing to note the frequency with which he brought money into his teachings about the Christian life.

Educational Factors

There likewise are educational factors in good financial policy. They, too, are important and should not be overlooked by church-school leaders in charge of budgets and finance. Those who guide the church school have opportunity to make of budget and finance a vehicle for education in the Christian's relationship to possessions. Factors important to Christian education are present in the following:

1. *The need for facts.* A thorough approach to our educational opportunity will include guidance for pupils in the *practical needs which the church and the whole Christian enterprise have for funds* with which to operate. Inescapably, organized religion is big business in a financial sense. No informed person questions the necessity for organized religion in today's world. Spasmodic, incidental, irresponsible giving is foreign to the realities involved. Responsible, planned giving, based on Christian motivation, is an educational goal. Let the people know why and for what money is needed.

2. *Plans of giving.* It is desirable that pupils be educated in possible plans of giving. Among plans commonly followed by Christians, three are noted:

a) Haphazard. Response to all worthy appeals without previous allocation of specified sums or proportions of the giver's resources is a procedure which has some worthy aspects. Its worth to the Christian enterprise, however, depends upon getting the appeals through to the giver and upon the reality of the giver's consecration and soundness of judgment. Though widely practiced, this plan hardly commends itself as the best way for the Christian to give, or as a basis for Christian education in stewardship.

b) Tithing. Tithing deserves much more thought and support than many have given it. As the minimum amount in a plan in proportionate giving (discussed below) it is scriptural. The sense in which it is scriptural should be the subject of careful education in the church school. Jesus' application of the principle is our sure guide. Clearly Jesus thought of the tithe as a working minimum, though the widow's mite was approved without any reference to the tithe.

A legalistic approach to tithing would specify the base upon which one tenth is figured, that is, whether gross income, income after taxes, net profit, or the like. A legalistic approach likewise would specify the causes for which the tithe would be given, often restricted to the organized church. We do not, however, support a legalistic interpretation of tithing. No one interpretation can be proved as *the* scriptural or *the* traditional one. It should be left to the individual tither to determine the base for figuring and the causes to be supported, church and others. But it is the responsibility of the church school, as it deals with tithing in its educational program, to make available what is known concerning scriptural and conditional background and to encourage an unselfish and consecrated determination of the matter.

We are indebted to Bishop William C. Martin for these Ten Basic Facts about tithing:

—Tithing is deeply rooted in a long history of observance in the Hebrew-Christian tradition.

—Tithing has satisfactorily met all of the demands that emerge from a complex industrialized civilization.

—Tithing is an outgrowth of a sense of thankfulness which, for the Christian, is as natural as breathing.

—Tithing lifts the financial support of the church from "what we feel like giving" to the level of regular, dependable, proportionate contributions.

—Tithing sets the economic pattern for the support of these institutions that undergird the moral and religious life of the social order.

—Tithing takes the irksomeness out of giving.

—Tithing puts a spirit of discipline into the handling of financial affairs.

—Tithing insures to the church and its agencies adequate and dependable financial support.

—Tithing imparts a special meaning and value to the nine tenths that remain.

—Tithing involves a continuous experience of adventure.

c) Proportionate giving. In this limited listing of worthy plans for Christian giving, the one designated "proportionate giving" merits enthusiastic support. Stated simply, it is giving in proportion to ability with ability determined in the light of conscientious Christian faith. There is good reason to encourage the proportionate giver to tithe as the minimum of his proportionate giving, and then to range upward from that as his ability makes possible.

Definiteness is encouraged. Though the proportion of assets set aside for giving may vary with the changing financial situation of the giver, amounts should be set aside from time to time and reserved for Christ's cause, through the church and through private and other worthy channels. Strict adherence to giving in proportion to ability leaves for individual determination the possibility of a level less than tithing for those desperately circumstanced. Some consider this questionable, however.

For the wealthy, proportionate giving often involves the continuous giving of large sums. But that is what "proportionate" calls for. The greater the ability, the greater the gift. At times true proportionate giving tests the integrity of persons of large financial means.

3. *Habits of giving.* In section 1, above, we noted the practical necessity of financial support for the church and other humanitarian enterprises. In section 2 we considered education in various plans of giving. We now come to a third educational factor, less detailed but surely as important, namely, education in the habit of giving. This, of course, is a part of good stewardship education. How can the habit of giving be encouraged and guided?

When one has knowledge of the needs which exist, plus a sense of responsibility deep enough to result in action, plus Christian faith and unselfish judgment to guide the sharing process, a person is in position to develop Christian giving into a habit. Making it habitual is then simply a matter of getting joy out of it and repeatedly doing it.

On every age level the church school can guide the growing person in all three of these ingredients. The guidance should be appropriate to the age involved. Indelibly impressing facts concerning financial needs for carrying the Christian enterprise around the world requires teachers to emphasize these facts as they occur in the regular lesson materials. It further requires the gathering of additional facts continually by keeping up with articles in the church periodicals. It involves interpreting to pupils what the work of the church is and what its financial program is. Far too many teachers know little or nothing about such things as local budgets, conference benevolences, world service, and mission specials. The director of stewardship education who is a member of the commission on education should take the lead through the commission on education in seeing to it that teachers and workers are informed.

4. *Participation in determining money use.* Thus far three major educational factors relating to finance in the church school have been discussed: guidance in understanding the need for funds, plans of giving, and habits of giving. There remains a fourth educational factor, participation in determining how the money is to be used.

Contrary ideas operate here.

On the one hand, the responses both of compassion and of liberality are stimulated by knowledge on the part of the giver about the causes that are to benefit. They often are stimulated further by opportunity to choose between causes. On the other hand, administration is vastly complicated and unattractive but worthy causes jeopardized when the giver stipulates exact causes his gift is to support.

Denominational finance, therefore, usually involves a dual approach. There is the general, main-line channel for giving which is administered by denominational officials to cover causes included in the denomination's financial undertakings. In addition there is provision for giving to designated "specials."

In the church school there often is provision for a triple approach. This takes the form of offerings for the church, the church school, and provision for retention of certain agreed amounts or proportions by a class or other unit to support causes undertaken separately by the class or unit.

Financial administration within a church school is simpler if all offerings throughout the church school go directly to the treasury of the church school to support its budget, but considerations more important than simplicity of administration are involved. Children, youth, and adults alike learn by doing. Stewardship motivation is strengthened and stewardship practices developed when the pupil, of any age, participates in the procedure all the way through. Ideally, this includes discovery or at least a knowledge of needy causes, determination of which causes are to be supported if it is necessary to choose between them, the giving of money and services (on a basis proportionate to resources), and a knowledge of what is accomplished by the gift. This makes evaluation possible.

This sort of participation would be close to the ideal embodied in the educational principle we are now discussing. Unfortunately, however, it is seldom possible for there to be such thorough participation by the giver in the whole process.

It is recognized that a good purpose is served, for instance, by junior age boys and girls having opportunity to retain some of their offerings in their own class or department to disburse for special causes which they themselves have selected. But it is equally good practice, and vitally necessary as well, that the church school as a whole be adequately financed and that an appropriate financial relationship with the local church as a whole be maintained. This calls for controls of some kind.

It is common practice for adult classes to support one or more causes of their own choosing. In addition, of course, they share in the financial support of the church and church school as a whole. While this practice of decentralized financial operations is deemed advisable if stewardship education is to be a reality, it can lead to difficulty if carried to excess. This illustrates further the need for controls.

It is the function of the commission on education to develop these controls. Not arbitrarily, of course, but reasonably. And reasonable control merits the co-operation of the classes and departments for the good of all. This control can work out in actual practice as follows:

a) Projects to be supported by classes or departments or other units in the church school are described, including length of time the commitments will run and the amount of money required to finance them, and the information is submitted to the commission on education. The commission approves or asks for modification and then approves, or disapproves. This approach is practical for major projects and should be followed. It is not practical for minor projects.

b) An agreement is reached between the commission and various church-school units as to procedure for retaining moneys in the class or unit out of offerings. The procedure may be to retain a percentage of all offerings. Or it may be to retain a cash amount each Sunday or period.

c) Each class or department or other unit may agree to underwrite a certain amount of the budget of the church school as a whole, remitting as may be agreed, and retain in their own treasury the balance of offerings received.

d) The relationship of offerings in the church school to the budget of the local church as a whole should be faced in the commission on education and governing policy developed. This gives further opportunity for stewardship education. This is discussed later in this chapter.

Relationship of Church School to Church Finance

Out of the multitude of different ways local churches handle church-school and church finance, it is doubtful if one plan has developed which could be called the best possible. But certain facts are clear.

One is that it is unwise for church-school finance to be swallowed up in church finance and its identity lost. It is equally clear that it is unwise for the church school to be completely on its own financially with no claim upon, or responsibility to, the church of which it is a part. Between these two extremes the proper relationship of church-school to church finance will be found. The following statements indicate such a relationship.

Basically church-school finance should be a part of church finance. As the "school of the church" the church school merits specific financial provision, whether the financial operations of the church are "unified" or not. An obligation rests upon the church to support its "teaching phase" financially, should there be need. Conversely the church school is obligated, should the situation call for it, to contribute to the financial support of the total enterprise of the church of which the church school is a part.

Knowledge of the financial operations of the church school should regularly be available to the official board and quarterly conference for counsel, should that be needed.

The individual members of the church school should be guided by the church school to participate in the financial support of the church. Education in giving to the local church is important just as is education in giving to causes outside the local church.

In the following section, under discussion of budgets, these relationships are illustrated.

Program and Budget Making

1. *Budget based on program.* That budget and program are related is clear. How they are related is another matter. There can be two answers:

a) Raise all the money you can then decide how much program it will pay for and make up a budget accordingly.

b) Determine the program that should be carried out, develop the budget needed, then raise the money to do the things the program includes.

The first of these is based on practical business acumen. The second is based on Christian faith. We can choose between them. Or better yet, we can draw on both of them.

Prudence dictates that we should not undertake more than we can pay for. But when Christian people understand what needs to be done in their church school, they are apt to find a way to pay for it. The basis of successful financing in the church school is not just in good business methods, though without good business methods we are in a precarious situation. The basis is in courageously, yet wisely, determining what

121

needs to be done (program), in acquainting the people about it thoroughly, and then in encouraging them as Christians to make it financially possible. That is, when we are dealing with faithful Christian people program-making comes first. Then budget is drawn up to cover. Then the money is subscribed to make it possible. But all is done within the realm of realism encouraged by faith.

2. *Developing the church-school budget.* On the pages which follow are guidance forms for determining the church-school program for a year. Exhaustive though this is, no standardized list can cover all possible local needs. Items will need to be added and items deleted. But the forms can aid in your program-making process. Your committee on general program, organization, and administration in your commission on education can do the basic work on this document, subsequently to be reviewed, revised if necessary, and approved by the commission on education. The pastor, the director, or minister of Christian education (if there is one), the director or minister of music (if there is one), each of the general officers of the church school, the three division superintendents, and each work area leader in the commission on education should have opportunity to offer suggestions for the year's program. Through the workers' conference, or otherwise, teachers and other workers should be encouraged to make suggestions. Program making should be a democratic process.

In the process many of the items in the guidance forms will need considerable amplification as, for instance, "Local Church Leadership Training Program," which here appears as only one line but which needs to be worked out in detail.

As the program-planning process goes forward, using these blanks, fill in the right-hand column where the money needed for the item is to be listed. Thus the budget-making process goes forward with the program-building process. Not all program items will involve money and hence will not be projected into the right-hand column.

On these blanks the program items are grouped to match the recommended committee structure of the commission on education, and it will be a simple matter to refer the various sections of the program to the various committees for amplification and final adoption by the commission, ready to be turned over to the superintendents, officers, and teachers for putting into effect.

The total of the cash listed will constitute the budget total for the year. At this point it is important that the various classes and departments have a complete understanding of the program proposed, what it will cost, and how much each must underwrite in order to cover the budget. If sufficient funds cannot reasonably be expected from the church school, the deficit may be covered by appropriation from the church budget. Only after every possibility has been faithfully explored should a wisely devised program be reduced in order to come within the funds reasonably expected to be available.

After approval by the commission on education the program and the budget should be made available as information to the official board and the commission on stewardship and finance.

3. *Achieving total program and total budget.* Just as there is a financial relationship between the church school and the church, so also there is a program relationship. Indeed, in a well-administered local church all phases of program throughout the whole church are related.

Administratively this can be brought about as follows:

Before the close of the church year the official board should devote at least one full meeting to the development of the total program of the local church for the succeeding year, based on the program elements provided by the commissions and other groups within the church. It should be the responsibility of the pastor and the chairman to arrange for this meeting and to insure that the commissions and other groups make advance preparation for it. This planning should be reviewed early in the new year and revised as needed.

This provision can be put into operation in the following manner.

After a date has been set for this program-planning meeting of the official board, all commissions and organizations in the church are requested, well in advance of the date, to prepare two things: (a) their proposed program for the year, and (b) their budget necessary to carry out the program. The forms on pp. 124 f. will help the church school in doing this.

When the program and budget forms have been prepared by all the groups in the church, they are assembled by a program committee composed of the pastor, the chairman of the official board, and the chairman of the various groups which prepared them. This program committee reviews and evaluates all program proposals. If advisable, it makes suggestions to the constituent groups for modification of program or budget, with special alertness for balance, conflicting dates, or inadequacies.

When all are in proper order, the program and budget proposals are put in the custody of the commission on stewardship and finance for presentation to the official board. In its annual program-planning meeting the official board then adopts both program and budget after such review as it deems wise. In reviewing programs and budgets from the

123

Church School
Program and Budget Builder Worksheet

Year ———————

THE COMMISSION ON EDUCATION
(Hand to Chairman of the Commission)

(Please read the following to the members of the Commission on Education so that all will understand.)

1. To do the planning that is involved, each member of the commission should have a copy of the *Manual for the Commission on Education* (8443-BC, available from any Cokesbury Store, 35 ¢).

2. This worksheet is to help the Commission on Education plan the program of Christian education for the church for the coming year and to determine what funds will be needed to put the program into effect. Check the columns which apply and on page 4 record any additional items needed.

3. These plans are to become a part of the total program of the local church which is being developed through the official board, with the co-operation of all the commissions and other groups in the church, as required by the *Methodist Discipline*, Par. 216.

4. As this worksheet is filled out, many program ideas will emerge for which there will not be space in this worksheet. Carefully record these for the detailed planning in which the commission will be engaged during the year. Only the main features of your year's program can be listed in this worksheet. Each of the work areas mentioned on pages 28 and 29 of the *Manual for the Commission on Education* will require detailed planning. This is discussed in the manual.

5. In connection with this planning of the total program of the local church, the church budget is to be developed for the coming year. The program and the budget will be used in the Every Member Canvass.

6. Under the *Discipline* (Pars. 233 and 266) the Commission on Education is responsible for developing and administering the budget of the local church school. Funds needed for the operation of the church school which are in excess of the amounts raised in the church school, should be provided in the church budget and made available for the church school. Space for requesting such funds will be found in this worksheet. In setting up the total financial operation of the local church and its organizations, the budget of the church school may be included as a section of the total budget exhibit without losing its identity.

7. This worksheet should be completed by ——————————————————. The chairman of the Commission on Education will then take it to the meeting of the program committee of the official board, where it is to be incorporated in the total program plans for the church. If it includes requests for funds from the budget of the church, it will also go to the Commission on Stewardship and Finance.

8. The pastor, the director or minister of Christian education, the director or minister of music, each of the general officers of the church school, the three division superintendents, and each work area leader (see *Manual for the Commission on Education*, pages 22-24) should have opportunity to offer suggestions for the year's program. Advance reading of the manual will be helpful in doing this.

9. In developing the program of Christian education in the local church the commission should be guided by good principles of program building. The church's program of Christian education should be based upon: (1) the needs and responsibilities of the people as recognized by the people, (2) the needs and responsibilities of the people as recognized by their leaders in the local church, and (3) the needs and responsibilities of the people as reflected in guidance coming from the Bible and the Christian heritage, and from district, conference, and general church sources. Through its program of Christian education the local church is endeavoring to provide for the people the guidance they need to accept and follow Christ as Lord and Savior, to serve Him as disciples working in the fellowship of His church, and to live daily as He would have them live.

10. On pages 2 and 3 of this worksheet the lines for entering estimated costs are designated by a letter and a number in parenthesis, as A(2). When pages 2 and 3 have been completed, copy on the left side of page 4 each of these cost estimates under the same letter on the line bearing the same number. This will automatically group the items under the conventional budget classifications. Complete the addition and you will have your total anticipated expenditures for the year. Then on the right side of page 4 list the sources and amounts of anticipated income, that is, the amount pledged by each department and adult class and other sources of income. The total of these entries will enable you to determine the amount (if any) needed from the church budget.

124

PROPOSED PROGRAM AND ESTIMATE OF FUNDS NEEDED FOR IT

The 13 numbered sections on these two inside pages correspond to the work areas on pages 30-59 of the *Manual for the Commission on Education* (8443-BC) available from Cokesbury at 35 ¢ per copy.	Check if planned for the New Year			Money Needed to Do It
	Will Start Doing It	Now Doing It Well	Should Do It Better	
1. Winning Pupils to Christ and the Church (Manual, pages 30, 31)				
Any recommendations from leader or committee in this area? Yes ☐ No ☐				
Annual meeting of the Com. on Ed. with the Com. on Memb. and Evang. present to plan year's church school evangelistic program..............				
An annual school of evangelistic teaching				$_____D (1)
Teachers informed and encouraged as personal evangelists..............				
Distribution and use of Teacher's Responsibility List...................				
Ordering and use of church-school evangelistic literature...............				A (2)
Full use of the Easter Season in church-school evangelism...............				
2. Recruiting and Training Leaders (Manual, pages 32, 33)				
Any recommendations from leader or committee in this area? Yes ☐ No ☐				
Discovery and enlistment of needed teachers and workers..............				
Local church leadership training program............................				C (3)
City, subdistrict or district training program........................				C (4)
Sending leaders to conference and other training centers...............				C (5)
Encouraging youth and young adults to enter church vocations...........				
3. Lesson Materials and Teaching Procedures (Manual, pages 34, 35)				
Any recommendations from leader or committee in this area? Yes ☐ No ☐				
Adequate provision for space for classes and groups...................				
Lesson and other material for all classes and groups..................				A (6)
Leaflets, manuals, and periodicals for all teachers and leaders...........				A (7)
Classroom supplies (paper, paste, crayon, minor equipment)				
General..				B (8)
Children's Division..				B (9)
Youth Division..				B(10)
Adult Division..				B(11)
Audio-visual equipment (projectors, speakers, etc.).....................				B(12)
Purchase and rental of audio-visuals (films, records, slides, etc.).........				B(13)
Books for the church school library................................				C(14)
4. Increasing Membership and Attendance (Manual, pages 40, 41)				
Any recommendations from leader or committee in this area? Yes ☐ No ☐				
An active membership cultivation superintendent (*Discipline*, Par. 143. 8)..				
An understanding throughout the church of the importance of increasing church-school membership and attendance......................				
Membership workers supplied with guidance literature.................				B(15)
Membership rolls and attendance records adequately maintained........				
A continual search for prospective new members, with adequate follow-up.				
Annual presentation to the commission of comprehensive plans..........				
5. Christian Stewardship and Giving (Manual, pages 42, 43)				
Any recommendations from leader or committee in this area? Yes ☐ No ☐				
All pupils taught the principles of Christian stewardship...............				
Tithing emphasized as a minimum plan of proportionate giving..........				
An annual budget for the church school.............................				
Adequate money handling procedures through the church school........				
Promotion of personal giving to church budget and related causes........				
Promotion and observance each fourth Sunday of World Service Sunday..				
Annual observance of Church School Rally Day with offering............				
Promotion of Methodist Youth Fund................................				
Promotion of Children's Service Fund...............................				

	Check if planned for the New Year			Money Needed to Do It
	Will Start Doing It	Now Doing It Well	Should Do It Better	

6. Missionary Education (Manual, pages 44, 45)
Any recommendations from leader or committee in this area?   Yes ☐ No ☐
Co-operative plans for missionary education of children and youth.......
Adequate use of mission study units, with particular reference to adults...
Special missionary programs in Methodist Sunday Evening Fellowship....
Co-operation with Com. on Missions in annual school of missions........
Encouragement of adequate and systematic giving to missions..........

7. Music in Christian Education (Manual, pages 46, 47)
Any recommendations from leader or committee in this area?   Yes ☐ No ☐
Supervision over the selection and use of music in the church school......
Insuring that all groups have hymn books which meet good standards.... ____B(16)
The integration of children's and youth choirs into church school.........
Music supplies... ____B(17)

8. Christian Service and Social Concerns (Manual, pages 48, 49)
Any recommendations from leader or committee in this area?   Yes ☐ No ☐
Program of Christian social service appropriate to each age group......... ____D(18)
Promotion of Christian interracial attitudes and activities................ ____D(19)
Familiarity with the Methodist Social Creed (*Discipline*, Par. 2020)........
Emphasis upon morals, world peace, and abstinence from drinking.........

9. Family Life (Manual, pages 50, 51)
Any recommendations from leader or committee in this area?   Yes ☐ No ☐
Study groups in Christian homemaking (*Discipline*, Par. 233)........... ____D(20)
Adequate guidance in the relationship of church and family............. ____D(21)
Observance of National Family Week (*Discipline*, Par. 250)............. ____D(22)
Application of family life guidance in (*Discipline*, Par. 2021) .... ____B(23)

10. Fellowship and Recreation (Manual, pages 52, 53)
Any recommendations from leader or committee in this area?   Yes ☐ No ☐
Cultivation of Christian fellowship throughout the school...............
Planning special recreation events, including outings, picnics, etc........ ____D(24)
Recreation equipment and supplies.................................... ____C(25)
Interchurch recreational activities.................................... ____F(26)

11. Christian Higher Education (Manual, pages 56, 57)
Any recommendations from leader or committee in this area?   Yes ☐ No ☐
Informing church on significance of Christian Higher Education.........
Informing church on Wesley Foundations and church colleges...........
Cultivation of support of these institutions in church budget.......... ____D(27)
Co-operation in the church observance of Race Relations Sunday,
   Methodist Student Day, and Student Recognition Day..............

12. Organizing and Sponsoring New Church Schools (Manual, pages 58, 59)
Any recommendations from leader or committee in this area?   Yes ☐ No ☐
Securing guidance literature from the General Board of Education....... ____B(28)
Understanding need for more church schools for growing population......
Review to determine if new church schools or outpost classes are needed.. ____B(29)
Discussion with the district supt. of plans for new church schools.......
Enlisting the co-operation of youth and adult classes and individuals.....
Enlisting the co-operation of the other commissions and the off. board....

126

	Check if planned for the New Year			Money Needed to Do It
	Will Start Doing It	Now Doing It Well	Should Do It Better	
13. General Program, Organization, and Administration (Manual, pages 54, 55)				
Any recommendations from leader or committee in this area? Yes ☐ No ☐				
Adequate organization of the Commission on Education.........				
Organization of the four parts of a church school (*Discipline*, Par. 243)...				
New classes and groups needed..............................				
Keeping up to date on the Christian education needs of the community...				
Guidance booklets from Gen. Bd. of Ed. (see catalog 542-B).............				A(30)
Methodist Church School Record System supplies.....................				B(31)
Employment of minister or director of Christian education or educational assistant (*Discipline*, Par. 143)................................				E(32)
Employment of secretary.....................................				E(33)
General furniture, equipment, and supplies....................				B(34)
Observance of special days designated for the church school: World Service Sunday (every fourth Sunday), Church School Rally Day, Children's Day, Promotion Day, National Family Week, Chris. Ed. Week....				D(35)
Weekday kindergarten.......................................				B(36)
Vacation church school......................................				B(37)
Day camping...				B(38)
Local church camps...				B(39)
Christian Adventure and Youth Activities Week..................				B(40)
Scholarships and delegate expenses to camps and conferences...........				F(41)
Commission, workers' conference, council, and committee expense........				D(42)
General promotion and publicity.............................				D(43)
Contribution to the church budget from the church school..............				G(44)
Miscellaneous items..				G(45)

several organizations the official board should not make revisions that have not been reviewed by the organization involved.

4. *Budgets—unified and otherwise.* This brings us to a consideration of the much discussed matter of a unified budget.

It will be recognized at the outset that the term is unclear. What one church means by a unified budget may not be at all what another church means. Putting "the benevolences" in the budget instead of raising them separately means a unified budget to some. Putting the church budget and the church-school budget together means a unified budget to others. Some churches achieve what they term a unified budget by simply gathering into one budget as many church interests as they can, including all special offerings. The special offerings are then discontinued as additional appeals.

Because of the wide differences which exist it is difficult to discuss briefly the advantages and the disadvantages of unified budgets. But certain observations can be made.

Convenience is often the justification of those who favor the unified approach. It seems to be easier to do the job and get it over with if every-

BUDGET YEAR_____

ANTICIPATED EXPENDITURES	ANTICIPATED RECEIPTS

ANTICIPATED EXPENDITURES

A. Lesson Materials and Literature

(2) $_____

(6) _____

(7) _____

(30) _____

Total $_____

B. Supplies and Equipment

(8) $_____

(9) _____

(10) _____

(11) _____

(12) _____

(13) _____

(15) _____

(16) _____

(17) _____

(23) _____

(28) _____

(29) _____

(31) _____

(34) _____

(36) _____

(37) _____

(38) _____

(39) _____

(40) _____

Total $_____

C. Recruiting and Training Leaders

(3) $_____

(4) _____

(5) _____

(14) _____

(25) _____

Total $_____

D. Promotion and Publicity

(1) $_____

(18) _____

(19) _____

(20) _____

(21) _____

(22) _____

(24) _____

(27) _____

(35) _____

(42) _____

(43) _____

Total $_____

E. Salaries

(32) $_____

(33) _____

Total $_____

F. Appropriations

(26) $_____

(41) _____

Total $_____

G. Miscellaneous and Contingent

(44) $_____

(45) _____

Total $_____

Total anticipated expenditures.......... $_____

ANTICIPATED RECEIPTS

From

_____ $_____

Total of above items.............. $_____

Needed from church budget to
balance anticipated expenditures... $_____

Total anticipated receipts.......... $_____

● ● ●

Department of General Church School Work
P. O. Box 871, Nashville 2, Tennessee
Division of the Local Church
General Board of Education of The Methodist Church
A World Service Agency

12-62   5 cents each   8484-C

Signed_____
          Chairman Commission on Education

Signed_____
          Church School Superintendent

thing is lumped together, "putting all the begs in one askit." Business efficiency likewise can be claimed. And a significant argument in favor of unifying the whole budget of the church and all its parts is the very point which is made concerning the relationship between the church and its church school, namely, that the church school *is* the church as the church engages in its teaching function. This being so, what is illogical about having one unified budget covering the whole church and all its parts?

Over against this point of view is the fact that centralization fosters an impersonal situation. The larger the church the more pronounced this can become. The causes for which money is given seem more remote from the people because, though not necessarily so, the sharing of information and cultivation often are not as thoroughly done. The total project involves so much detail that it is difficult, and sometimes tedious, to keep the details in the picture as the budget is presented to the people.

That the people should have the detail is beyond question. The financial aspect of the church is not simply a matter of getting persons to give money to pay bills. Response to the stewardship ideal is an important Christian function. The giver is not simply responding to pressure to give up some money for a cause vaguely understood to be worthy. At its best, church finance is the expression of the Christian's deepest motivation, sacrifice for a vividly present cause. So there is justification for keeping the people involved in understanding and deciding and often in initiating individual, detailed causes.

What then can be done to preserve the values in the two opposing points of view concerning budgets? Fortunately there is an answer.

In the immediately preceding discussion (p. 123) each organized group in the church in effect developed a budget or a proposed budget at the time it developed its program for the year. At that point there existed a proposed "church" budget and a budget for each of the constituent groups, including the church school. The suggested procedure (p. 127) brought all these separate financial exhibits together, with the programs envisaged, to the official board as information and for review.

At precisely this point there is opportunity to achieve a desirable degree of unity without cancelling out the values in the separate approach.

Let each separate financial exhibit (budget) coming from the several constituent groups be preserved as finally agreed upon. Do not lump them all together. Make up the total budget of the church by placing side by side the several organizational budgets. For instance, each could have a separate page in the total budget exhibit of the church with a page, of course, for the general budget. The total of all of these is the total of the whole church budget, but the integrity of each part is preserved.

Where this plan is followed it is possible to have for the entire matter one set of books, one bank account, one bookkeeper, and one treasurer. Thus the economies of a unified approach are achieved. But each part is set up separately in the total system, and the accounting is kept separate. This sort of thing is common practice in a business firm which maintains separate funds within a total bookkeeping system.

Several additional observations are in order.

Funds are withdrawn from the separate budgets within the whole only on requisition of the group whose budget it is. For instance, only the authorized officials in the church school could draw money out of the church-school funds. This would be done by a requisition on the central treasurer, who would then issue a check chargeable against the church-school budget.

Less clear, however, is the matter of how money given by the individual member is handled. Probably there would be little support for the plan of "everyone giving to everything" by dividing all receipts on the ratio which the various constituent budgets bear to one another, and crediting the proper percentage to each budget. The alternative is to have all receipts clearly designated and credit them to the budget for which they are intended. For illustration, money coming from the church school for the church school would be credited to the church-school budget.

This plan can work regardless of the size of the church.

A variation from this plan holds possibilities attractive to some. When the several group programs and their accompanying budget exhibits are before the official board (see p. 123), instead of setting up a centralized bookkeeping system with one bank account and a total (though compartmentalized) budget, the several program and budget exhibits can be returned to the several constituent organizations in the church and each handles its own finances. The values in having the official board observe the total program and financial plans of all organizations are still retained, but beyond that there would be no centralization.

Records and Routines

1. *Financial records.* Financial records in the church school are, of course, kept in various ways. Perhaps the way is not too important, providing they are kept in accurate and understandable fashion. But these elements are needed in the financial records: (*a*) pages for recording and crediting offerings and other receipts and for recording disbursements;

(b) the treasurer's cash account which would include check book and bank balances, deposit slips corresponding with the cash entries in the general book (see first item above), and vouchers corresponding with checks issued (voucher envelopes which contain requisitions and cancelled checks are simple to use); (c) a comparison of receipts and expenditures with the budget to keep track of finances as authorized in the budget; (d) adequate financial accounting in each class or department which retains money for its own projects; (e) adequate financial reports to the commission on education and to the official board.

2. *Routines for handling money.* Routines for handling money should be developed and maintained. "Who transmits what to whom" should be clearly understood, and there should be no deviations from the routines. This would include channeling offerings from class (or group) to department to general secretary (or treasurer) to bank. Procedures for authorizing expenditures should be clearly established including authorization for signing checks.

3. *Custody of funds.* The custody of funds would be established as the above routines were worked out. In some instances the general secretary receives the offering money brought in from the various classes and groups, deposits it in the bank, and gives bank deposit slips to the treasurer as evidence of deposits made. In such cases only then are funds in custody of the treasurer. Church-school money invariably should be kept in a bank, and remittances should be made only by check. The one exception to this is not, in effect, a real exception because checks finally are involved. The reference here is to setting up "petty cash boxes" for departments or groups needing to make small purchases from time to time. A check for a modest amount issued to an individual for "petty cash" would be converted into cash and the cash kept in a box or envelope. As small purchases for supplies and the like are made from the cash, receipts or memos showing amount and nature of transactions would be put in the box or envelope. The "petty cash box" should always be in balance, that is, it should always contain the original amount, figuring receipts and memos as the equivalent of cash for accounting purposes. As the amount of cash gets low in the "petty cash box" the receipts and memos are presented to the treasurer who, where authorized, issues a new check to cover. This is converted into cash and placed in the "petty cash box" thus restoring the original amount in the box. The treasurer's check issued to cover the receipts and memos would be posted against the proper items in the budget.

4. *Function of treasurer.* The function of the treasurer varies in different church schools. Typically, the treasurer in addition to being

custodian of funds is a very valuable officer in keeping the commission on education and the general officers informed as to the financial position of the church school. But occasionally a treasurer assumes responsibilities which are not vested in him and undertakes to control expenditures. In this a treasurer is overstepping the normal bounds of his office. He is custodian of funds, but how they shall be spent is determined not by the treasurer but by those authorized by the commission on education to make those decisions. All persons handling any considerable sums of cash should be bonded. Usually the church as a whole has provision for bonding treasurers, and those in the church school should be included in the plan.

5. *Audits.* Audits of all accounts throughout the church school are necessary and should be had at least annually. This is the responsibility of the commission on stewardship and finance.

The Secretary of Stewardship and the Church School

Each year quarterly conference should elect a "secretary of stewardship." He should be a member both of the commission on stewardship and finance and the commission on education. His central responsibility would be cultivation and promotion of Christian stewardship, and his leadership in the work of both commissions could help the local church significantly in the vital area of stewardship.

Being a member of both commissions and thus intimately involved in guiding the operations of the church school, the secretary of stewardship is in position to draw on the resources of the commission on stewardship and finance for the enrichment of the program of stewardship education and giving in the church school. Similarly, because of his connection with the commission on stewardship and finance, the secretary of stewardship can help relate the church school to the general program of stewardship promotion and cultivation going on in the local church under the commission on stewardship and finance. These interrelationships can result in strengthening the total stewardship activities of the local church.

In the organization of the commission on education it is suggested that the secretary of stewardship serve as the leader of the work of the commission which comes under the heading "Christian Stewardship and Giving." And if the commission is organized into committees, the secretary of stewardship could serve as the chairman of the committee on stewardship and giving in the commission on education.

Working through the commission on education, the secretary of stewardship can do the following things:

1. Help the leaders throughout the church school recognize that there is a relationship between commitment to the Christian life and giving to the church and other Christian enterprises. This can be discussed in workers' conferences and teachers' meetings.

2. He can help the church school face squarely the matter of tithing, interpreting tithing as a minimum plan of proportionate giving. Many of our people do not understand tithing, and the secretary of stewardship can help at this point.

3. Through calling attention to the stewardship elements in the regular lesson materials and by supplementing them with special guidance as may be needed, the secretary of stewardship can help in creating an understanding that money consecrated and given for Christian work can be thought of as the giver spending himself for that cause. Money thus given becomes an extension of the giver and involves the giver in the Christian enterprise being supported.

4. There is definitely a stewardship element in the observance of special days and occasions which include offerings. It is appropriate that the secretary of stewardship do all he can to interpret these observances in terms of Christian stewardship.

5. In developing the budget for the church school the secretary of stewardship can be of great help. Indeed, this help can extend to the entire financial program of the church school. There is a relationship, of course, between the church-school budget and the total budget of the local church, and the secretary of stewardship can interpret this relationship, seeing to it that in financial matters, as in all other matters, the church-school budget not lose its identity within the total of the local-church finance.

6. The every-member canvass of the local church should be related to the general program for the local church, and no one is in better position than the secretary of stewardship to guide the commission on education in co-operating in its execution and in other financial aspects of program making.

7. In the church school there should be frequent programs on Christian stewardship in order that stewardship education be strongly embedded in the program. For instance, the Sunday evening fellowship offers admirable opportunity for programs from time to time lifting up Christian stewardship ideals. There can be study classes in Christian stewardship conducted during the week. The secretary of stewardship, as a member of the commission on education and intimately involved in the operations

in the church school, is in position to exercise leadership in full utilization of program opportunities within the church school for further stewardship education.

A Statement of Financial Policy
for the Church School

At the beginning of this chapter it was stated that a pattern would be given for a policy statement covering church-school finance. It was suggested that such a statement should appear in the records of the commission on education and should be available to the official board and to the commission on stewardship and finance. The following statement of financial policy was developed for a particular Methodist church school, but is applicable to church schools in general:

A Statement of Financial Policy
for the Church School

Date————————————————

Sec. 1. Financial provisions shall be made for the total Christian educational work for which the commission on education is responsible, that is, the church school which includes—
   a) Sunday School
   b) Methodist Sunday Evening Fellowship
   c) Weekday Activities
   d) Home and Extension Service

Sec. 2. The financial operations of the church school shall be in harmony with the provisions of the *Discipline* as follow:
   "¶ 233.7g. [The commission on education shall] plan the financial program of the church school [including the requesting of funds, if needed, through the Commission on Stewardship and Finance], budgeting all church-school funds and giving careful supervision to expenditures.
   "¶ 266.5. When causes are combined in the [church] budget, the budgetary responsibilities of the Commission on Education and the church school, as stated in ¶ 233.7g, shall not be contravened."

Sec. 3. Financial matters shall be administered and the teaching of stewardship shall be conducted in such a way as to emphasize the spiritual factors involved, including the highest Christian motives for giving.

Sec. 4. While full responsibility, within the abilities of the school, shall be undertaken for providing funds necessary for conducting the school, financial matters shall be so handled as to preserve the educational factors involved. This shall include education in the financial needs of this church school and church and of the Christian enterprise around the world, education in plans of personal giving in an effort to achieve

134

the highest in Christian practice, and education leading to making such giving a lifetime habit.

Sec. 5. In determining annually the financial program of the church school the commission on education shall proceed in harmony with the best interests of the church as a whole and as occasion arises shall seek the counsel of the official board in matters involving the financial relationship of the church school to the church. The responsibility of the church school to the church and of the church to the church school shall be recognized.

Sec. 6. Annually before the beginning of the fiscal year, and in harmony with the procedures for developing the total budget of the church, the commission on education shall prepare a budget for the church school. The budget shall be based upon the program which the church school purposes to carry out. As an aid in this preparation the Program Builder Worksheet for the Commission on Education should be consulted [see p. 124].

The budget shall show in detail anticipated income from offerings and appropriations and anticipated expenditures and shall be in balance before it shall be accepted by the commission on education.

A temporary committee, consisting of the church school superintendent (chairman), the church-school secretary and treasurer, and the three division superintendents, shall prepare the proposed budget for submission to the commission on education.

In preparing the program and the budget each department in the children's and youth division and each class and group in the adult division (including the four parts of the church school as indicated in Section 1) shall be given opportunity to make suggestions. And each shall indicate the amount it will undertake to provide through its offerings during the year in support of the budget.

Every effort shall be made by the church school to underwrite its budget through its own offerings. In event this does not prove possible the commission on education shall request the commission on stewardship and finance to make the needed amount available from the church budget. In event the church school is able to establish a surplus in offerings over the amount needed for the church-school budget, it shall report that fact to the commission on stewardship and finance and make such surplus as accrues available to the church budget.

There shall be consultation by representatives of the commission on education with the officers of each adult class and the appropriate departments or divisions in the rest of the church school concerning

135

the way in which the budget shall be supported through offerings. In event a portion of the offerings is retained for group projects (see Section 15) there shall be a specific agreement about the rest of the offering. These options are available:

    a. The group may undertake to provide a stated amount each week for the budget, retaining the balance for their own projects (see Section 15).

    b. All offerings may be divided on a ratio stipulating the portion for the budget and the portion for group projects.

    c. The group may devote all offerings to its budget commitment until the commitment is met; then for the rest of the fiscal year retain all offerings for projects.

At least once a quarter there should be review of the way budget commitments are being met by each group. In event of shortage the church-school budget has priority over group projects.

The church school shall not carry over any unappropriated funds on hand beyond the end of the fiscal year, unless by special arrangement with the commission on stewardship and finance, but shall release such surplus to the church. Adult classes and all other groups and departments are requested to conform to this, releasing surpluses at the end of the fiscal year.

The church-school budget, after being perfected and approved by the commission on education, shall be transmitted to the commission on stewardship and finance as information for that commission and the official board.

Sec. 7. The financial records of the various classes, groups, and departments shall be kept in a clear and business-like manner, using the books and blanks in the Church-School Record System. The financial records of the church school as a whole shall be kept in the *General Secretary-Treasurer's Record Book* of the Church-School Record System in conjunction with whatever system of centralized bookkeeping may be employed by the church.

Sec. 8. All financial records throughout the church school shall be audited annually by the commission on stewardship and finance.

Sec. 9. Policy established by the official board shall govern the bonding of treasurers in the church school.

Sec. 10. (If the local church does not have a central accounting system and a central treasurer for the church as a whole, including the church school, the following shall govern:)

    Offerings and other funds received for the church school (exclusive of funds retained as described in Section 15) shall be received and

136

recorded by the church-school general secretary and shall be deposited promptly by ——————————— to the account of the church school in ———————————————Bank with a duplicate deposit slip furnished to the church-school treasurer. Disbursements shall be by check only, signed by ————————————and only on authorization of ————————————, except that there shall be provision for petty cash expenditures as described in Section 11.

(If the local church does have a central accounting system with a central treasurer for the church as a whole, including the church school, the following shall govern:)

Offerings and other funds received for the church school (exclusive of funds retained as described in Section 15) shall be received and recorded by the church school general secretary and transferred to the central treasurer in the manner prescribed in the plan for centralized accounting for crediting to the budget and the accounts of the church school and for bank deposit as the plan may provide. Disbursements of funds budgeted for the church school or otherwise controlled by the church school shall be upon requisition only, signed by ———————————————, who has been designated by the commission on education as having the authority except that there shall be provision for petty cash expenditures as described in Section 11.

Sec. 11. As may be authorized from time to time by the commission on education and notation thereof be appended to this document, division and department and other officers in the church school may be given petty cash amounts, under the following provisions:

  a) Authorization shall be to specified persons for specified amounts.
  b) Check for petty cash shall be issued to the person for the amount specified and that person shall be responsible for the custody, the disbursement, and the accounting for the amount involved.
  c) With the cash thus provided, the specified person may purchase minor supplies and make small expenditures within policy limits which the commission on education may establish, thus relieving the central treasurer of issuing small checks for incidental expenditures.
  d) As petty cash is paid out, itemized receipts or memoranda shall be preserved by the person having custody of the petty cash so that at all times the remaining cash, plus the receipts and memos, will equal the original amount of the petty cash check.
  e) Annually before the close of the fiscal year, and as often as there is need (within the budget allowance) for cash in the petty cash fund, the accumulated receipts and memos should be presented for a requisition on the treasurer who will issue to the specified

137

person a check for the amount of the receipts and memos thus restoring the original cash amount in the petty cash fund. The receipts and memos shall be posted against the proper items in the church-school budget.

f) In closing out a petty cash fund for a particular person, follow the procedure under "e" above, and then receive from the person his check for the original amount of the petty cash check. This will close out this particular petty cash transaction. All petty cash funds shall be closed out before the church-school treasurer's books are closed at the end of each fiscal year, and then re-established for the new fiscal year, if there is need.

Sec. 12. The routines for handling offerings throughout the church school shall be as follow:

a) Class, group, or department secretaries shall be responsible for receiving the offering.

b) The amount of the offering shall be entered on the weekly report to the general secretary, itemized as called for on the report form.

c) In event a portion of the offering is retained for projects of the class or group or department (see Section 15), the amount of that portion, as well as the balance sent to the general secretary, shall be entered on the report form and the balance of the cash, together with the report form shall be transmitted to the church-school general secretary.

d) The class or group or department secretary shall post in the back of the book of blanks, the full details of this cash accounting, as the permanent record of the class or group or department.

e) Upon receipt of the offering the church-school general secretary shall check the cash with the entries on the blank and copy the data into the *General Secretary-Treasurer's Book.*

f) Amounts retained by the class or group or department under the provisions of Section 15 shall be in the custody of the class or group or department treasurer for banking or, in the case of very small projects, personal keeping.

Disbursement authorization shall be clearly established and records shall be kept for auditing as provided in Section 8.

Sec. 13. For the quarterly report to the official board and the quarterly conference the church-school secretary shall supply the financial data required, showing receipts and disbursements in relationship to budget.

Sec. 14. The secretary or treasurer shall report monthly to the commission on education showing receipts and disbursements in relationship to budget, including a statement as to amounts retained by classes, groups, and departments under Section 15.

Sec. 15. It shall be permissible for classes or groups or departments, after meeting their responsibility to the budget of the church school, to retain a portion of the offerings they receive for projects of their own, under the following conditions:

a) It is desirable that initiative and self-determination be approved and encouraged on the part of groups in the church school, in terms of their maturity, with respect to group projects financed by the group. It likewise is desirable that an equitable balance be preserved between such projects and the budget of the church school as a whole. Further, it is recognized that the commission on education must exercise the degree of supervision that may be needed to maintain that equitable balance.

b) It, therefore, is requested that classes and groups desiring to commit themselves to one or more continuing projects involving financial expenditures, make available to the commission on education, through their division superintendent, information as to the nature of the proposed project and the amount of the financial commitment. This would be as information, or for review and suggested modification if the purposes and effectiveness of the church school as a whole would be compromised by the project.

c) Classes and groups are encouraged, in terms of their maturity, to maintain modest sums available for emergency donations to alleviate suffering for appropriate courtesies and for nonrecurring causes which cannot be anticipated and handled as a project. It is not suggested that detailed information concerning such expenditures be furnished to the commission on education unless requested.

d) It is requested that annually before the close of the fiscal year each group retaining funds from its offerings and as provided in this section report to the commission the total retained from offerings and the total expended, analyzing expenditures into projects, courtesies and emergency relief. This need not be detailed. The report should show any cash balance on hand and indicate what portion, if any, is reserved to meet a designated obligation. Unappropriated balances should be released to the general treasury of the church school to be turned over to the church as indicated in Section 6, above.

Sec. 16. The fiscal year of the church school shall be ————————.

9

ORGANIZATION, GRADING, AND GROUPING

Two Observations About Organization

As consideration is given to the subject matter of this chapter we refer to a point of view stated earlier in the book: Because the church school is actually the church itself engaged in Christian teaching, the church school is not in itself an organization. But it *has* an organization in order to get its work done. Realization of this helps to keep things in perspective. Organization is important only as it serves.

There is a second fact which emerges here. Organization is directly related to educational philosophy. The way of teaching which governs in a given church school requires an organizational pattern suited to it. And when we get to the chapter on Building and Equipment, it will be equally apparent that the design and arrangement of the physical plant which houses the teaching operation must likewise be consonant with the approach to teaching which is employed.

Three Elements Involved

There is first the question of the grouping of the members themselves. Is our traditional age grouping sound? Can the idea of a children's division, a youth division, and an adult division be maintained? If so, how can it best be expressed? If not, what would be better?

Second, there are the activities in which the members engage and the organizational structures needed to make the activities possible. Will these conform to age-group patterns? Or cut across them? Or will there be some other approach?

And third, what provision is needed to get the planning done? What groupings of leaders are needed to insure adequate program and proper conduct of Christian educational processes? And what about our clearer and clearer focus on the nature of leadership in Christian education? The long-held notion that we have leaders and we have followers and that all we need to do is put people into their pigeonholes and all will be well has turned sour. These facts have bearing on the organizational structure needed for planning.

It would be easy, but shortsighted, to throw together a conventional organization and hope it would serve a yeasting and rapidly changing concept of what Christian education really is. All in all we have a neat problem ahead of us as we consider organization, grading, and grouping in a modern church school.

These three elements will be considered in some detail on the following pages.

Grouping, Age Groups, Learning Groups

We could quickly dispose of the matter of grouping by repeating what the past has bequeathed us. Whether we accept it or reject it, we had better be familiar with it. Here it is:

Traditionally there are four basic groups of persons in a church school.
1. The general officers and over-all leaders
2. The adults
3. The youth
4. The children
The adult division includes persons about 22 years old and over. There is not usually a departmental organization in the adult division. The working units

are adult classes and groups. Usually there are age differentiations as between classes or groups.

The youth division includes persons 12-21 (about) years old. Depending on the size of the church, there are departments within the division and classes and groups within the departments. In very small churches the whole division may constitute only one department. Medium-size churches may have two departments. Large churches usually have three departments, thus:

Junior High (ages 12-14)
Senior High (ages 15-17)
Older Youth (ages 18-21)

The children's division includes persons from birth to 11 years old. As in the case of the youth division, the size of the church usually determines the department and class grouping. Conventionally, the maximum provision has been:

Nursery Department (ages 0-3), including
    Nursery Home Roll
    Nursery Group
    Nursery Class
Kindergarten (ages 4-5)
Primary (ages 6-8)
Junior (ages 9-11)

All of the above is further discussed on page 145.

But were a church school to settle permanently for the above, thinking it was making provision for contemporary developments, it would soon find itself involved in a maze of exceptions, as is pointed out below. While it is true that the above is still the age-grouping pattern used in many, probably most, of our present church schools (though only a portion are large enough to use the complete pattern), it cannot be said that this represents the best in modern educational thinking. This will be discussed further later on.

Here is part of the difficulty:

The 21- and 22-year-olds have much more in common than do, for instance, the 12- and the 20-year-olds. Yet these latter are often in the same division while the 21- and 22-year-olds often are not. At best the dividing lines between divisions are arbitrary. They can be defended only on the basis of custom and of convenience. Our language provides us with three age designations: childhood, youth, and adulthood. Yet there never has been complete agreement as to where one ends and the other begins. Were we in position to wipe the slate clean and start over again with no presuppositions to which we had to conform, with our present knowledge it is hardly probable that we would set up three major age groupings. Why not four? Or five? An older-youth young-adult division

142

is a strong contender for acceptance, and one denomination is definitely planning to make two separate divisions out of the 0-11 year group (see p. 145). This breaks the three-division pattern. As we learn more about conducting Christian education, there is less to cause us to conform rigidly to these traditional divisions.

Of course the traditional divisions can be defended as a convenient scheme for administration. They do divide the members into units for handling, and we have become accustomed to them. And, frankly, there is no point in discarding them until we are convinced that there is something better. We are in the questioning stage, experimenting with new ways, but not all of these new ways have proven themselves. Those who guide a church school do well to keep open minds at this point.

Do we need both a division and a departmental grouping? Indeed, do we need *either* a division or a multiple class department grouping? As will be discussed in the next chapter, most new buildings, if they reflect current thinking in design for Christian education, have "self-contained" classrooms where an age group of children, and often youth, of one or two year span spend the entire period. Adults have long followed the plan of remaining in "their room" for the entire period. We hear less and less about occasions which bring all of the members of a large three-year department together. Gatherings of the whole membership of divisions and even of departments are going the way of the "opening and closing exercises" of the whole school. That is, they are ceasing to exist.

Should grouping of children be by ages or by public school grades? Should adults be grouped by ages or by interests, with classes and groups formed around topics with opportunity for individuals to realign themselves from time to time? Is there any place in a modern church school for grouping by sexes? What can be said for the idea that favorable learning takes place in groups that cut across age lines (for instance, family groups), as well as in groups that adhere to age lines?

In the midst of change and consequent uncertainty, how does a responsible administrator catch hold? He may be alert to new developments and interested in new theory, but next Sunday he will be dealing with real people in a real building and probably with some very real traditions and habit patterns. What does he do? Happily, there are some guide lines which he can follow.

The first is that he probably should do nothing at all about this next Sunday. This is not a matter for crash programs.

The second is to be aware of what is going on. By reading the denominational magazines and publications, and by reading some of the books constantly referred to in them, he can keep in step with emerging knowledge. He can attend training schools and take courses in church-school administration. This is a continuing process and can be started at any time.

The third is to be familiar with the denominational curriculum. The lesson material is planned to be used in certain specific ways. For instance, materials written for team or group teaching can hardly be used in a situation where one teacher sits in front of five or six listless pupils and "teaches by telling." And this has bearing on age grouping and on organization. As the church-school administrator comes into an adequate knowledge of modern curriculum throughout the school, the newer designs for grouping and for organization will normally unfold for him.

The fourth is to study the physical plant, the floor plan and the arrangement and the equipment, along with the number of members and the present and potential leadership, in the light of what is being learned about age grouping and organizational structure. That is, put all factors together and arrive at reasonable solutions based on the local situation.

The foregoing is good generalization. Can't guidance be made more specific? Let's try.

First, the basic question about having the sexes together or separate in classes and other groups. For many years the prevailing judgment has been to keep the sexes together throughout the entire church school, including all ages. The only exceptions are specialized groups such as Boy Scouts. Yet one continues to find, even in well-planned church schools, some separation by sexes, chiefly in the adult division. What should be done about this?

A good rule seems to be: (a) do not organize any new classes or groups on a sex-segregated basis; (b) get children's and youth classes and groups on the combined basis as rapidly as possible; (c) if existing sex-segregated adult classes can readily be converted to the other plan without undue opposition, make the change as opportunity can be found; (d) leave undisturbed venerable adult classes that do not want to change.

The designation of children's classes and groups by public-school grades is increasing in favor. Likewise, the tendency to have more departments with fewer grades in each is observable. Indeed, where classes are self-contained (remaining as a group in their room for the entire period) and include only one or two public-school grades, the significance of "departments" depends more on administrative convenience than on educational requirements. On pp. 141 f. the conventional grouping pattern is outlined. For quick reading this, and some modern variations from it, is expanded below. Unavoidably this listing is incomplete. Considerable experimentation is under way. One denomination is announcing a complete regrouping of children beginning in 1964.

Children (birth-11 years, or sixth grade) :
In the *small church* there are these possibilities for Sunday school:
    4 to 7 or 8 years of age, usually called the children's class
    9 to 12 years of age, usually called the boys' and girls' class
If the church has as many as six to fifteen children in any of these groupings, classes should be formed as follows:
Nursery class—3 years of age
Kindergarten—4 years to first grade
Primary—Grades 1, 2, and 3; ages 6, 7, 8 years
Junior—Grades 4, 5, and 6; ages 9, 10, 11 years
In even the smallest church the possibility for a nursery home group should be explored as well as Sunday evening and weekday groups, as discussed later in this chapter.

In the *large church* there are these organizational possibilities for children:
1. Four departments
    Nursery department—including (a) nursery home roll for babies served by the nursery home visitor, (b) a nursery group for two-year-olds, and (c) the nursery class for three-year-olds
    Kindergarten department—children 4 years to first grade
    Primary department—grades 1, 2, 3; ages 6, 7, and 8 years
    Junior department—grades 4, 5, 6; ages 9, 10, and 11 years
2. The two-year plan
    Nursery department—including (a) nursery home roll for babies served by the nursery home visitor, (b) a nursery group for two-year-olds, and (c) the nursery class for three-year-olds
    Kindergarten department—4 years to first grade
    Primary department—grades 1 and 2; ages 6 and 7 years
    Primary-Junior department—grades 3 and 4; ages 8 and 9 years
    Junior department—grades 5 and 6; ages 10 and 11 years
3. The grade plan
    Nursery department—including (a) nursery home roll for babies, served by the nursery home visitor, (b) a nursery group for two-year-olds, and (c) the nursery class for three-year-olds
    Kindergarten I—four-year-olds
    Kindergarten II—5 years to first grade
    Primary I—grade 1
    Primary II—grade 2
    Primary III—grade 3
    Junior I—grade 4
    Junior II—grade 5
    Junior III—grade 6

One of our large denominations, planning a completely new children's curriculum, intends to separate into divisions what formerly was one division, which will give them a younger children's division and an elementary division. And they are seriously considering attaching nursery activities to the adult division.

For children's groups the following sessions should be provided:

Regular Sunday-school sessions of one to three hours

Additional sessions for primary and junior children on Sunday or weekday (may be part of the Sunday evening fellowship)

Frequent weekday gatherings for day camp, choirs, recreation, and other activities

Denominational or co-operative weekday religious education

Vacation schools for kindergarten, primary, and junior children

Youth (12-21 years, or beginning with seventh grade—the upper grade may be modified as needed)

In the *small church* there are these possibilities for Sunday school: At least two classes, one for boys and girls 12-14 (junior high) and one for senior high and post high (15-21). If there are as many as six junior highs and a number of older youth, consider a department organization as suggested for the larger church.

And in the *small church* several of these youth activities usually are possible:

Worship and study in the Sunday school

Worship, fellowship, discussion programs, and special activities as a part of the Sunday evening fellowship

Business, socials, recreation, mission study, evangelism, worship, and service projects on weekdays

Youth-serving agencies such as Scouts, Campfire Girls, if they are under direction of the commission on education

The regular Sunday worship services of the church

All-church services, activities, projects

Contacts with homebound youth and those away at school, work, and in military service (home and extension roll)

Subdistrict, district, conference youth activities

In the *large church* there are these organizational possibilities for youth:

Junior-high department—ages 12, 13, 14 years

Senior-high department—ages 15, 16, 17 years

(Some group the 12-17 age span into three 2-year departments. Some put older youth and young adults together.)

Older-youth department—ages 18-21 years

You may combine some of these in this way:

Junior-high department—ages 12, 13, 14 years

Senior-older youth department—ages 15-21 years

And in the *large church* these youth activities usually are possible:

Worship and study in the Sunday school

146

Sunday evening worship, fellowship and discussions, and special activities on Sunday evening—as a part of the Sunday evening fellowship where it is held

Weekday meetings for business, socials, recreation, mission study, evangelism, worship, and service projects

Denominational or co-operative weekday religious education

Youth-serving agencies, such as Scouts and Campfire Girls, if they are under the direction of the commission on education

The regular Sunday worship services of the church

All-church services, activities, projects

Contacts with homebound youth and those away at school, work, and in military service (home and extension roll)

Subdistrict, district, conference youth activities

Adults (22 years and older—the lower age may be modified as needed)

In the *small church* these groups are suggested—

One or more Sunday-school classes. If possible, three—young adults, middle adults, and older adults. A church school, small or large, that does not include adults seriously handicaps the progress of its church.

Even in the small church there can often be study groups of adults during the week, as well as a group of adults in the Sunday evening fellowship.

And practically every small church can have a group of home members.

For the *small church* these adult meetings usually are possible in the church school:

Sunday-school classes for study and discussion

Groups in the Sunday evening fellowship

Through-the-week groups for older adults

In the *large church* these groups are suggested—

A large number of adult classes and groups serving young adults, middle adults, and older adults will prove very advantageous. Give thought to specialized short-term classes and groups to meet special needs and opportunities.

Adult home members and adult extension members should form an important part of every large church school.

In the *large church* these adult meetings should be scheduled as a part of the church school:

Sunday-school classes for study and discussion

Groups in the Sunday evening fellowship

Weekday groups for special interests, socials, learning for life schools

In all church schools, small and large, the participation of all members in all the activities of the church appropriate to their age should constantly be encouraged.

Organization for Activities

The foregoing section related to age grouping of the members. We consider now the second of the three basic elements in church-school

147

organization, the activities in which the members engage. The activities are comprehended within the four parts suggested for the modern church school, namely: (*a*) Sunday school, (*b*) Sunday evening fellowship, (*c*) weekday activities, and (*d*) home and extension services.

If these four separate enterprises were only loosely associated under the covering term "church school," we could organize each of them separately and be done with the matter. But they are not.

Our approach to organization must be to the church school as a whole. If we fail to approach the matter this way, we undercut the unity that must characterize this total Christian educational enterprise of the local church. The parts are all under the control of the commission on education, all are served by the workers' conference and the three age-group councils, and all serve the three age divisions.

This unity can easily be illustrated. There is not a youth organization for the Sunday-school hour, another youth organization for the Sunday evening fellowship hour, another for weekday activities, and another for home and extension services. Instead the youth of the church constitute the youth division of the church school, and that youth division operates throughout the four parts of the church school. The same is true for the children's division and for the adult division. And it would be true were a different grouping by ages employed in place of the conventional three.

This makes possible a unified program of Christian education for any given age group and, indeed, for any given individual. The Christian education which the local church offers a given age group, or a given individual, can all be under one total plan and program. How disconcerting it would be to an individual if what he got at Sunday school had no relationship to what he got at Sunday evening fellowship, and if what was offered him by the church during the week had no relationship to the other two.

Persons old enough to recall the days of the youth Sunday evening "society" (Epworth League, Christian Endeavor, and the like) will recall that those Sunday evening activities had no relationship, either in program or in organization, with anything else that went on in the church for those same persons. Long ago the Protestant churches of America recognized the inadequacies in such an arrangement and, in varying degrees, have moved toward a total, unified program and organization to serve a given age group.

So it turns out that when we consider the organization of the four basic activities of the church school, we will do the job as a unit and not as four separate organizations.

One church-school superintendent should lead them all. One set of general officers—secretary, treasurer, membership cultivation superintendent—should serve all four parts.

Here we often witness a breakdown of progress. The lesson of experience and the beckoning of a validated ideal bring us to a recognition of the solid worth of a unified plan for Christian education in our local churches. But often we find our way blocked. Sometimes it is blocked by the dead hand of the past. Some are still living in the "Epworth League" days. They conform to new terminology but in their minds the Sunday evening youth group is just as separate from Sunday school as it was fifty years ago when the League and Christian Endeavor were in their prime.

Sometimes our way is blocked by laziness. "Why not be content just to have a Sunday-school class and let it go at that?" Or, "A Sunday evening group is about all we can manage in this community. No real need for more." Or, "Let's let 'em do as they please. If somebody wants to start a Sunday evening group, that's all right with us. Sunday school is all we can take responsibility for."

Yet in this fast moving, competitive day when many voices and many involvements lure the people away from the church, we cannot stop short of the best we know. The best that modern Christian education knows is to plan as a whole, not piecemeal and unrelatedly, the Christian teaching which the church offers the people. And the organizational outcome of unified teaching is unified organization. Within that unity there can and should be variety. Sunday evening fellowship does not duplicate the experiences of Sunday school, and during-the-week activities differ from both. But all are complementary parts of a unified whole. This whole we call the church school, which is the name we give to the church as it engages in Christian teaching.

What are the characteristics of a unified approach to organization that includes the suggested four parts of the church school? Here are some quick glimpses:

1. An authoritative planning group (commission on education) responsible for the entire enterprise

2. A workers' conference which includes all leaders throughout the whole church school

3. Division councils which include key leaders serving their age groups throughout the whole church school

4. Division and department groupings which are maintained through all parts of the church school

5. General officers who likewise serve the entire enterprise, but who may have

assistants who have specialized responsibilities within any of the parts of the church school

6. A budget which covers the whole church school

7. A concept of membership which causes a person who is related to any or all of the parts of the church school to be identified not just as a member of a Sunday-school class or of a Sunday evening or weekday group, but also as a member of the church school, that is, of the Christian educational enterprise of the local church.

Stated another way, a contemporary church school does not have a Sunday-school organization, an evening fellowship organization, a weekday organization, and a home and extension organization. Instead, the organizational features of the church school as a whole operate through all of these parts.

The general officers are the general officers of the whole affair. Specifically, under this concept of organization there is no such officer as a "Sunday-school superintendent." That term went out of use when the inclusive church-school idea emerged. The proper title is, of course, "church-school superintendent." The person holding that office is the administrative officer of the commission on education. The commission on education is responsible for all parts of the church school. And the church-school superintendent naturally is superintendent over all parts. The same is true with the other general officers.

The three age-group divisions (children's division, youth division, and adult division) are not just divisions of Sunday school. They function through the entire church school—Sunday evening, during the week, and in the home and extension service as well. The division officers and the division organization extend through the whole enterprise. The same is true of departments within the divisions.

But when we reach the class and group level this no longer holds true. The class grouping for Sunday school seldom is maintained in the Sunday evening fellowship or in the weekday activities. Within the divisions and departments there is change in the basic groupings (classes and other groups) to meet the differing situations Sunday morning, Sunday evening, and during the week. The group alignment for Sunday school may be by ages or school grades, while for Sunday evening fellowship it may be according to interests that cut across age lines.

Further consideration of classes and groups may be helpful. If popular usage is a guide, we find approval for both stability and flexibility. It remains true that the organized class, particularly with adults and youth, is very much a present reality. In the opinion of many the organized class is the solid foundation on which the church school rests. Not all agree. But in any event, it must be recognized that it has a place.

But likewise there is widespread and enthusiastic approval for periodic change in class and group structure. Dynamic things are happening where older youth and adults are given opportunity to regroup themselves, as often as once a quarter in many cases. On a planned schedule a variety of study opportunities are available from which the individual may choose. This practice is not limited to the large church.

In the children's division particularly, but not limited to children, team or group teaching gives wide opportunity for variety within the group structure. In such a group there is little that is kin to a static organization. Flexibility and constant accommodation to the changing requirements of curriculum characterize such a group.

A disturbing question persists. Desirable loyalties can cluster around a continuing, stable class or group. Members find their real attachment to a group of persons. In a situation which fosters frequent changes in grouping, what happens to those loyalties? The answer is that while class loyalty becomes less of a factor, there can be loyalty to a larger group which is wholesome and effective. But it is not automatic and is harder to maintain. The department or division must be more in evidence and good public relations and unfailing attention to the individual member are imperative. Fortunately, the disturbing question thus has an encouraging answer.

Organizational Provision for Planning

The third element considered in this chapter is the provision, in terms of organizational structure, necessary for *planning the work* of the school. Before us for discussion are the commission on education, the division and department councils, and the workers' conference. The focus here will be on organizational structure rather than function and program. Of course, function should dictate structure.

The Commission on Education

It should be noted at the outset that some churches are so small that it hardly seems possible to have a commission on education, or commissions on anything else. For such situations two suggestions are made.

1. It can be assumed that the quarterly conference can elect a chairman for each commission including, of course, the commission on education. Even in the very smallest church we would hope to have a class for adults, one for youth, and one for children. The three teachers could function as "division superintendents" and thus would be available for

the commission. Perhaps one of the three has been designated as chairman and another as church-school superintendent. These three persons could function as the commission on education and do the planning needed for this very small school. And there may be other ex-officio members available.

2. Or in the very small school another approach is possible. The person elected by the quarterly conference to be chairman of the commission on education is a member of the official board, as are all the other commission chairmen. Also on the official board are other church-school leaders including the church-school superintendent. At stated times let the members of the official board meet and function as the commission on education, under the chairmanship of the person elected to be chairman of the commission on education. (The same procedure can be followed for the other commissions in the local church.) And lest someone suggests that it would be simpler for the official board, as such, to take over and do the work of all the commissions since the same persons are involved anyway, be it remembered that what is everybody's business is nobody's business, and having a separate chairman for each commission will likely insure better attention to the work of each commission as its turn comes.

But such a very small church is not the normal situation. Normally, we have a regular commission on education. How, then, should a regular commission be organized?

It already has a chairman, selected annually by the quarterly conference. So to complete its list of officers the commission has only to elect from its membership a vice-chairman, a secretary, and a librarian and literature secretary. It is not to be overlooked that the commission also selects the teachers and group leaders (except teachers of adult classes elected by the classes, subject to confirmation by the commission) and representatives from its own membership to serve also as members of each of the other commissions. The other commissions likewise select representatives to be members of the commission on education.

Will the commission on education have committees to help get the work done? Let that be decided by the commission. Here are possibilities:

Subject to change if local needs suggest another approach, it is felt that every church school should work in the thirteen areas listed on pp. 125 ff.

Very large church schools could have within the commission on education a standing committee in each of these fields. Since this would tax the capacity of most church schools, there are simpler approaches. One is to assign more than one area to a committee. Another is to raise these committees from time to time to study and recommend programs to the commission. When its recommendations for the year have been considered, the committee can be discharged for the rest of the year and its members released to serve in other ways. Still another way is to have committees of one member. Each would become well-versed in his field and lead the deliberation of the commission when program is being perfected.

It is to be noted that the representatives from some of the other commissions on the commission on education could serve admirably as leaders for certain of these areas. For instance, the representative from the commission on evangelism could guide the planning for Winning Pupils to Christ and the Church.

Thus there unfold a number of suggestions for the organization of the commission on education.

Division and Department Councils

Little in the way of organizational structure is needed. The division or department superintendent usually serves as chairman. As needed, a secretary may be selected, with special committees from time to time. Usually informality is wise in the procedures of these groups.

Workers' Conference

The church-school superintendent should serve as chairman, with program leadership being provided as called for by the program. If a secretary is desired, the church-school secretary can serve or one can be selected. Special committees will be needed from time to time, but probably no standing committees, with the possible exception of an agenda committee including the church-school superintendent (as chairman), the pastor, the three division superintendents and the director or minister of Christian education—if there is one.

As this chapter is concluded, the two suggestions with which it opened are repeated.

1. The church school is not in itself an organization. It has an organization to make its work possible, but organization is subordinate to purpose. The church school is the church organized for its teaching task.

2. The educational philosophy which governs the school should type the organization of the school and all the elements composing it. The alert church school progresses in organization as well as in program.

10

BUILDING AND EQUIPMENT

In our growing nation those who guide church schools frequently find themselves involved in building programs. Similarly, more or less extensive remodeling of existing buildings is commonplace. What do such persons need to know about the design and equipment of the building that houses their church school? This chapter undertakes to present information related to that question.

Some General Observations

Perhaps the most important information needed is that denominational headquarters stand ready to help. Specifically, the general board of education offers technical assistance, largely in outlining procedure, that is invaluable to the local church-school leaders. At best it is shortsighted not to use this help. At worst it is little short of criminal, one is tempted to say when he sees some of the monstrosities that are designed by amateurs on a do-it-yourself basis. Church-school buildings last a long time. The errors that are heedlessly made can handicap succeeding generations to a distressing degree. There is a way to avoid this. At the very outset get in touch with your general board of education and ask for guidance.

Ranking in importance with guidance from denominational headquarters is the decision to employ a competent architect, even for a small building with modest financial outlay. Money "saved" by not paying for an architect often is paid out many times over in blunders which are permanently built into the structure. A volunteer draftsman—even when combined with a building contractor who is donating his profits to the church—seldom can take the place of a competent architect skilled in church-school design.

Then this, which may seem to contradict the paragraph you have just read: Even the best architect needs guidance from the local church-school leaders. Every church-school building, if it is to serve well, must be individually designed for the particular situation. Church-school buildings are not cheaper by the dozen. Local factors will influence design, and the architect will need many facts from the church-school leaders. The more the local church-school leaders know about the factors which enter into good building design, the better able they will be to provide the information needed by the architect. The remainder of this chapter is devoted to such factors.

Program Should Determine Design

Someone has written of the necessity to "break the tyranny of outward appearance dictating inner arrangement." The commendable desire to have a beautiful looking building (and all church-school buildings should be in good taste and suggest that which is holy) can lead the inexperienced to a wrong approach to design. They are apt to begin with the outside and work toward the inside. The proper procedure is to design the building from the inside out.

Another way of saying this is, program should determine design. Those who understand good procedure do not build a building and then fit the program to the building. Instead, they decide what is to take place in the building (that is, program) and then they construct a building that is designed to help carry out that program. The architect needs to know what the building will be used for—and in great detail. He then can design a structure to house the program. This is basic.

155

That is why it is incorrect to start with a building committee that turns immediately to design. The beginning point should be with a program committee that will determine in detail what is to be done in the building.

Teamwork

In the design, erection, and equipping of a modern church-school plant, professionals and volunteers work together. Certainly there must be professionals. These are the skilled advisers in denominational headquarters whose counsel should be sought, the architect who has had successful experience in church-school construction, and the building contractor whose skill, facilities, and integrity mean so much in good construction. The volunteers are the wise, experienced leaders in the church school who spend long hours learning the kinds of information their professional teammates will need, and who carefully determine what is to go on in the building not only today but tomorrow and on into the future. The volunteers also are the loyal leaders of the entire local church who oversee the project, arrange for its financing, and who provide a setting in which the church-school leaders can make their contribution. And, of course, among the volunteers are those who uphold the project with their prayers, their encouragement, and their money. It takes teamwork to build a church-school building.

Looking Ahead

With tragic frequency one finds instances of failure to recognize that the future must be considered as well as the present. Bighearted church leaders recognizing that the church school needs a new building, proceed by the shortest route to get it. Organizers of new churches, commendable for their Christian zeal and sacrifice, put through a building program which includes the church school, but sometimes with little or no consultation with their Christian educators. These fine people grew up in Sunday school, but it does not occur to them that a new day has dawned in housing Christian education and that the future will bring still more changes. They know about changes in the scientific world, but more often than we could wish it does not occur to them that change likewise characterizes the educational world.

A permanent structure should never be built for the present. The present is too brief. Building should always be in terms of the present and the future, because the physical plant will last far into the future. Those who design a building for the church school must know the trends and how to evaluate them, must know the direction progress is taking, not only in Christian education but in the local community as well. The admonition to look ahead should constantly be in the minds of those who determine the design for a church-school building.

Functional Design

The generalization "Decide on your program and then build a building around it" calls for specifics. One is that church-school building design should be functional. The function of the various parts of the building, the precise use to which they will be put, should dictate the way they will be designed. For instance, will the program of the church school include provision for retarded and physically handicapped persons? Will teaching involve a larger use of audio-visual equipment? Will ability to look out through windows be a factor in the program for any age group? Will it be advantageous to have ready access to outdoor areas, grass plots, open patios? If, in your program as you project it into the future, the answer to questions of this nature is yes, your new building must be so designed that these functions can be performed—it must be functional.

Flexibility

It often happens that in a changing, growing situation guiding principles do not exactly mesh. Sometimes they contradict. We have been considering the principle of functional design. That means exact application of design to specific intended use, with resulting specialization. Now we come to another guiding principle, that of flexibility, which crashes head-on into the principle of functional design. Or does it? We must work our way around this somehow. But first we will look at the idea of flexibility in design.

The meaning of this is simple. A room assigned today to a junior-high group may be assigned five years hence to an over-65 group as a part of reassignment of space to reflect changing conditions. To meet this possibility the room should be so designed that the change in use will require a minimum of change, if any, in the physical structure.

A building in which use assignments can be changed with a minimum of inconvenience to program, is a building with a flexible design. The desirability of this is apparent. Christian education is not an exact science. Teaching is a changing, growing thing. What it will be ten years from now cannot be stated positively, except to say that it probably will be different. But even more pressing is the fact that our age groups will

157

vary in size and in needs from period to period during the life span of the building. To be able to reassign space is highly desirable.

Consider the case of the nursery room that had elephants and clowns and a whole menagerie cast in bas-relief in the plaster of the walls. Highly entertaining! (That is, for the adult workers; it probably did not register at all with the kids.) But seven years later, after the philanthropist who sired and financed the idea had died, the room as assigned to the choir for rehearsals! If only the elephants could have been hung by wires instead of being cast into the plaster!

Also consider this. At an extra cost of seventeen dollars each above standard price, child-size toilet fixtures were installed liberally in the portion of a new building assigned to small children. Further, the toilets were accessible only from the rooms occupied by the children's groups, not from the corridors. That was functional. Everyone was delighted. But less than a decade later needed additions to the building necessitated reassignment of space, and older youths were put in those rooms. The plumber's bill to install new fixtures was not the main difficulty. The chief problem was limited access to the toilets.

Here are instances of functional design blocking flexibility. Both are desirable. What do we do?

In these particular cases there is an easy solution. Don't bring elephants into the building in the first place, and there is a growing resistance against installing cute little child-size fixtures. Children do not have them at home. Use sturdy, safe, removable step-ups instead. And arrange for corridor access to toilet rooms with a minimum of changeover when space is reassigned.

But these are special cases, and such easy solutions do not generally emerge. The desirability of reassigning space is almost inevitable during the life span of a building so the idea of flexibility is sound and should be maintained. Must we, then, abandon functional design in order to achieve flexibility?

Fortunately, the answer can be "no" if, in designing a functional building, extreme specialization is avoided. A building has functional aspects if the proportion of length to width in rooms is good (2 to 3 or 4) and if rooms are sufficiently large (400 to 600 square feet on an average, with 300 and 700 square feet as the extremes). Functional design avoids excessive stair climbing in any case—whether for little children or older adults or for the in-betweens. Likewise, weight-bearing partitions are avoided to the greatest possible extent, so that needed later changes can be made with a minimum of difficulty. Wide corridors and well-planned traffic flow contribute to functional design, and if these features are present throughout the building, reassignment of space will never result in traffic jams at any point. On the other hand, if one's philosophy of age-group specialization in Christian education requires that window sills be at one height for children, another for youth, and another for adults, then that is that. That is an illustration of a narrow application of function blocking flexibility.

Sometimes a choice has to be made. But in the main the two principles can be followed in a building if there is not too much insistence on close specialization.

Multiple Use of Space

Church schools that have two and even three sessions of Sunday school each Sunday morning are no longer unusual. So the idea of multiple use of space is introduced into the thinking of those who design church-school buildings. Few problems would arise were both (or all three) of the Sunday-school sessions identical as to age groups and approximate numbers. But seldom is this absolute uniformity encountered. Variations frequently result not only in *multiple* but also in *different* use of space. This is another reason for the desirability of broadly flexible design so that a given part of the building can be assigned to more than one use.

But multiple use has an additional application in the modern church school, that is, the same building and at least some of the same rooms must serve for Sunday school, for the Sunday evening fellowship, and for weekday activities. This fact must be considered in the design and equipment of the building.

And, too, modern usage often calls for the entire building to be occupied at the same time. That can mean noise problems unless this total usage has been anticipated and appropriate soundproofing employed as may be needed.

Self-contained Classrooms

Modern design calls for abandonment of the idea of departmental units consisting of a large assembly room with a number of small classrooms adjoining, which some years ago were considered desirable. Instead, the present requirement is for rooms large enough to contain a group who will remain together during the entire period (Sunday school, or Sunday evening, or weekday). And such large rooms are equally usable by children, youth, or adults.

The reasons for this change include: Good Christian educational procedure no longer calls for a period of formal worship in larger groups, followed by a "class period" during which the pupils are divided into smaller groups taught by one teacher. Formal worship is assigned to the sanctuary in connection with the "preaching service." That is, it is no longer planned that Sunday school alone will provide a complete experience, but both Sunday school and the worship service of the congregation in the sanctuary are required. Informal worship is integrated into the class period of a larger group in a self-contained classroom. Contemporary lesson materials are designed for the larger self-contained classroom experience.

Further, team or group teaching has so thoroughly validated itself in experience that both the lesson materials and the design of the building reflect this newer procedure. This is true for all ages. And the larger, self-contained room is designed for this newer approach.

The Handicapped

Not infrequently toilet doors are narrower than the standard doors throughout the building. Consider the problem this causes persons in wheelchairs. But should a building be designed just for the few who must come in wheelchairs? The answer is "no" and "yes." "No" in the sense that extreme accommodation to unusual needs would be irrational. "Yes" in the sense that for very little additional cost many things can be done which will make it possible for the handicapped to participate.

Stair climbing does not receive a thought from the young and the physically well persons. But in the average congregation there are some who have heart difficulties. Perhaps the reason they have not been observed at church and church school lately is that a flight of stairs is to them as great a barrier as a locked door. Modern design avoids stairs wherever possible. Ramps frequently solve problems for wheelchair occupants.

Age Distribution

Flexible design reduces, but often cannot completely eliminate, the necessity to determine the number in each age range to be accommodated in the building. And even though much of it is movable, much of the equipment is designed for a particular use. Practical considerations do, therefore, indicate the wisdom of an appraisal of the number in each age range to be served.

Unfortunately, in some American communities custom decrees that adults not participate in Sunday school. They may take part in other phases of the church school, but not in Sunday school. In such communities there is a temptation to design the church school for children and youth only. That is unwise. Perhaps the liveliest, most exciting element in education today—religious and secular alike—is adult education. To conclude that custom, though of long standing in a community, will permanently block Christian education for adults is unwise. Changes are taking place. Statistics indicate that in some denominations there are more adults in church school than either children or youth. And each year nearly half a million more are added to the over-65 group in America.

Your general board of education will have helpful suggestions for you as to procedure in arriving at decisions about age distribution, not only as to number in each age range, but as to location in the building as well.

Equipment and Storage

Especially for the younger ages equipment is a factor of increasing importance. And because of the variety and volume of it, a detailed discussion of it is not practical here. Your general board of education is in position to suggest in detail what is needed and sources from which it can be secured, including a do-it-yourself approach attractive to many church schools. As is apparent, there is a close relationship between lesson materials and equipment. Indeed, equipment becomes a part of curriculum—broadly conceived. Hence the imperative necessity for those who guide a church school to be alert to equipment needs.

The variety of equipment, as well as the desirability of keeping it possible to reassign rooms should the future make that wise, argues against built-in storage for equipment. Built-in shelves and bins and cabinets were once thought to be most desirable in church-school design. But no longer. Design such storage to accommodate the equipment that will be used, but avoid fastening it to the walls if at all possible. Keep it portable. A certain amount of built-in closet space is desirable in rooms for any age and purpose, but even this can be overdone where space and financial resources are limited. Provide adequate equipment and adequate storage for equipment, but keep in mind the possibility of moving it to another room at some future date or of changing it to conform to some future new approach to teaching procedure. The late, scarcely lamented vogue for built-in worship centers scattered indiscriminately throughout the building, but now hidden behind screens much of the time, illustrates the point.

Floor Space

The Christian educator is tentative in his approach to procedure and to standards for building design and space assignment. The reason is that things change in this field. New insights emerge. New understandings of the application of Christian teaching to a swiftly changing world enter the picture constantly. So it is hard to pin the Christian educator down in these matters.

But the architect and the building contractor cannot be tentative. Concrete and steel and stone and wood do not lend themselves to "whereas" and "that depends." Precise decisions must be made and the construction allowed to proceed.

Nowhere is this problem more evident than in the changing ideas about the number of square feet of floor space needed per person in a church-school building.

It can be said, however, that the changes have consistently been increases. Those who are leading our thought in this matter realize the mounting cost of providing enough space per person to do good Christian education, but they have not been inclined to compromise. Sometimes the building committee does, and forces the teachers and leaders to work under less than the best circumstances. To encourage as liberal an attitude as possible in providing enough space the following table is suggested as fairly representative of requirements at this period in the developing procedures of Christian education.

Group	Recommended Square Feet per Person		
Nursery (1st yr. crib, 2nd yr., 3rd yr.)	.35 (good);	30 (fair);	under 25 (poor)
Kindergarten (4th yr., 5th yr.)	.35 (good);	30 (fair);	under 25 (poor)
Primary (1st, 2nd, and 3rd grades)	.30 (good);	25 (fair);	20 (poor)
Junior (4th, 5th, and 6th grades)	.30 (good);	25 (fair);	20 (poor)
Junior High (7th, 8th, and 9th grades)	.25 (good);	15 (fair);	12 (poor)
Senior High (10th, 11th, and 12th grades)	.25 (good);	15 (fair);	12 (poor)
Older Youth	.25 (good);	15 (fair);	12 (poor)
Young Adult	.20 (good);	15 (fair);	10 (poor)
Middle Adult	.20 (good);	15 (fair);	10 (poor)
Older Adults	.20 (good);	15 (fair);	10 (poor)

Partitions

A visitor was being escorted through a new church-school building by the proud pastor and the custodian. They came to a long narrow room having three doors into the corridor and equipped with two folding partitions. Eagerly the pastor explained that this flexible arrangement enabled them to push back the two folding partitions and use the space for large gatherings, or to pull the folding partitions across to give them three square classrooms. But to the chagrin of the pastor the blunt custodian added, "Yes, but we can't use the middle classroom because of the noise."

This is not an isolated case. One encounters it again and again as he visits church-school buildings using folding partitions.

Experienced church-school designers specify folding partitions very sparingly, if at all. A partition should be a barrier both to sight and sound. If the barrier is not to exclude sound, movable screens are cheaper. And long narrow rooms that can hopefully be divided into classrooms are not functional in their undivided state. They are tell-tale indicators of poor design.

Miscellany

Many, many more things press for consideration, such as heating, ventilation, air conditioning, administrative centers, wide corridors (safety and fellowship), provision for drama, audio-visuals, drinking fountains, hats and coats, acoustics, lighting, color, floors, maintenance, parking space, future expansion, partitions (when will they invent a soundproof one?), and so on. These illustrate the fact stated at the beginning of this chapter. It was that perhaps the most important thing for a church-school leader to know when a building project is impending is that the denomination's general board of education should be consulted. There rich resources await your inquiry. Your architect will thank you if you use this resource liberally. And your teachers and workers will bless you for it.

11

JOB ANALYSES

       Effective operation of a church school requires that each officer, teacher, and worker understands what his responsibilities are. That is self-evident. This chapter undertakes to suggest specific, detailed descriptions of the responsibilities commonly associated with the general offices in a church school. But in using this material difficulties will be encountered.

    The first is that in a church school precise procedures are seldom possible and frequently are inadvisable. A church school is not a machine. It is not a military organization. Its purposes are divine and it is basically supported by a greater power than man, but it is operated by very human individuals. Undoubtedly the best in method and in job description still awaits discovery. The degree to which leadership resides in the group is a factor in determining job description. It is not just a matter of an individual taking over and getting the job done. Yet, a practical philosophy of mutuality in policy making and administration includes the fixing of definite responsibilities in specific individuals.

A second difficulty in developing job descriptions is that a church school is a voluntary enterprise using untrained leadership whose services are not constantly available. Further, the leaders themselves are in a process of growth and vary in degree of spiritual maturity and in leadership ability. This results in the advisability of a high degree of mutuality and shared responsibility among leaders, and much bearing of one another's burdens. Clear distinctions between jobs are not always possible. Overlapping is not only inevitable but often desirable.

A third difficulty resides in determining the point at which detail and sheer bulk of responsibilities overwhelm a volunteer worker and do more harm than good. It is unrealistic to confront a new office holder in a small church school with a list of duties that would tax the abilities of a full-time professional worker.

In assembling the material for this chapter the intent has been to be reasonably thorough and to present aspects in detail with the thought that the material will be a source from which to draw in developing job descriptions in a specific church school. No list will fit all church schools. But items which reflect successful experience may prove helpful to a church school in working out its own.

Chairman of the Commission on Education

1. *Serves as an example* to the commission in faith, consecration, and work so that through the church school the teachings of the Master may be taken to the people.
2. *Understands the total organization* of the local church and how the commission on education co-operates in the total purposes of the church.
3. *Understands the work of the commission* on education, that it is the policy-making and governing authority covering the total educational program of the local church, and that the entire church school is under its charge.
4. *Serves as chairman* at meetings of the commission, understanding that he is a *presiding* officer, not an *administrative* officer. (It is the church-school superintendent's job, not the chairman's, to administer and carry out the decisions of the commission.)
5. *Sees that the records of the commission are kept.*

6. *Secures effective functioning* of the commission by:
   - holding regularly monthly meetings and at the scheduled hour
   - promoting full attendance and full participation at meetings
   - making it possible for pastor, superintendent, director or minister of Christian education, director or minister of music, and other workers to exercise leadership in the commission.

7. *Develops the agenda* for meetings (in consultation with pastor, superintendent, and director) following some such order of business as this:
   - prayer
   - introductions and courtesies
   - approval of previous minutes
   - unfinished business
   - reports and statements
   - new business
   - miscellaneous
   - adjournment with prayer

8. *Presents for consideration items selected* from the fields of work of the commission (see p. 89). He does this from time to time in consultation with the pastor, superintendent, and director. Ultimately every field should receive full attention.

The Church-School Superintendent

1. *Is executive officer of the commission on education.*

   The commission on education is the body responsible for the church's program of Christian education. It plans and oversees the entire matter. The church-school superintendent is responsible for seeing that the plans and actions of the commission are carried out.

2. *Understands the operation and relationships of the commission on education.*

   As executive officer of the commission who counsels with its chairman and assists in developing its agenda and guiding its work, the church-school superintendent must understand the purpose and operation of the commission, and how it relates to other phases of the work of the church.

3. *Knows the basic fields of work in which the commission on education guides the church school:*
   - winning pupils to Christ and the church
   - recruiting and training leaders
   - lesson materials and teaching procedures

166

- increasing membership and attendance
- Christian stewardship and giving
- missionary education
- music in Christian education
- Christian service and social concerns
- family life
- fellowship and recreation
- general program, organization, and administration
- Christian higher education
- organizing and sponsoring new church schools

4. *Is chief officer of the church school.*

The church school includes all the Christian educational activities of a local church. It has four main parts:

- Sunday school
- Sunday evening fellowship
- weekday activities
- home and extension service

The church-school superintendent is the chief officer of this entire enterprise, and under the commission on education is basically responsible for its successful operation.

5. *Knows the community and its needs.*

The church school should be evangelistic and aggressive. It should reach out to serve the community spiritually, not simply exist for those who come. Its mission is to bring the teachings of the Master to the people. To accomplish all this the church-school superintendent must understand the community, know the kinds of people in it and what their spiritual needs are. The program of the church school should be tailored to fit.

6. *Understands the basic purposes of Christian education.*

To lead those who engage in Christian education, the church-school superintendent must himself know what it is. He must know the part played in Christian education by the imparting of information, by the influencing of behavior, by the surrendering of a life to Christ. He must see that lives changed toward Christ is our goal—rather than minds merely stored with holy facts.

7. *Knows the curriculum materials of the denomination.*

This includes not only the items used Sunday by Sunday, but also the additional resources available, including audio-visuals, to which he can turn for enrichment and betterment of teaching procedures. The lesson material prepared and approved by the denomination is extensive and versatile. From it can be selected what is needed by various groups in various stages of development.

8. *Knows why the denomination's materials should be used.*

It is not arbitrary to require denominational church schools to use denominational lesson materials. There are reasons for it, such as:

- It is planned and produced by and for the denomination.
- It is based on the denomination's point of view.
- It undergirds a definite program of action.
- It is subject to denominational supervision and direction.
- It creates loyalty to the denomination.

Lest the above be interpreted as supporting "denominationalism" in the unacceptable sense, it should be realized that co-operating strong denominations are an asset, not a liability, to ecumenicity. It is the strong denomination with loyal members, not the weak one, that makes the greatest contribution to united efforts to Christianize the nation.

As between free choice of curriculum material reflecting no denominational position and no denominational loyalty, on the one hand, and conformity to the denominational position in its Christian teaching, on the other, there should be no uncertainty. Denominational loyalty, within reasonable bounds of Christian thought, is desirable. If a church school questions the curriculum material supplied by its denomination, the corrective is to operate within the denomination and bring about changes as prove wise. There are two additional considerations here. One is the question of the competency of local leaders to judge the doctrinal and the educational adequacy of curriculum materials. This is a highly complex and scholarly business. The other is the proved hazards, educationally and doctrinally, of using literature from commercial suppliers.

9. *Knows the pamphlet material available.*

The general board of education issues lists of booklets and pamphlets. These cover in detail the whole range of organization, administration, and programing. In them will be found helps in solving practically any problem a church-school superintendent faces. He should be familiar with them.

10. *Understands the function of the workers' conference and his relationship to it.*

The workers' conference includes all officers, teachers, and workers

in the whole church school. Whereas the commission on education develops policy and basic plans and oversees the whole church-school enterprise, the workers' conference exists for these purposes:
- to promote fellowship, inspire and build morale among the church-school workers
- to give information and opportunities for study
- to discuss and develop the work planned by the commission on education
- to make recommendations to the commission

The church-school superintendent is chairman of the workers' conference. Agenda for meetings is developed by the church-school superintendent in consultation with pastor and other church-school leaders or arranged by a committee of which the church-school superintendent is chairman.

11. *Is leader—not dictator.*

The wise church-school superintendent sees to it that the church school is staffed by competent leaders. He then delegates to them as much responsibility as possible. He works through the three division superintendents and the membership cultivation superintendent, not usurping their authority, but inspiring, guiding, and assisting them. He likewise establishes practical working relationships with the pastor, the chairman of the commission on education (and the director or minister of Christian education, if there is one), with each knowing the part he is to play on this important "first team." He understands and uses the democratic process. He inspires initiative and creative activity from all leaders and teachers.

12. *Sees to it that the school has the needed teachers and leaders.* This will require:
- The development by the commission on education of a comprehensive and continuing plan to meet all needs involved:
    a) discovery of proper persons who could serve
    b) enlistment of those discovered
    c) training of all teachers and workers
    d) maintenance of the teaching force at full strength and efficiency.
- The fixing of responsibility for carrying out the plan. A committee from the commission on education is often used. Usually the division superintendents are involved in discovery and (after clearance) enlistment. Training and maintenance involve many phases, carried out in many ways.

169

13. *Insures the co-operation of the church school in the great tasks of every local church (evangelism, education, missions, finance, Christian social concerns).*

Evangelism. (Evangelism in the church school is thought of as commitment to Christ as Savior and Lord and joining the church.)

- Sees to it that the church school is evangelistic through and through.

    a) Has the commission on education develop a plan for training teachers to be evangelists:
    —orientation of all new teachers so they will understand what is expected of them
    —utilization of guidance literature prepared for this purpose
    —wise emphasis through workers' conference
    —an annual school of evangelistic teaching

    b) Insures diligent administration of the plan.
- Checks on actual progress.
- Co-operates with the pastor and commission on evangelism in church-wide evangelistic projects.

Education. (This whole job analysis covers this.)

Missions.

- Missionary education is an important part of Christian education. Emphasis is to be given to missionary units in the regular curriculum and to special missionary programs from time to time.
- Special mission study groups of children and youth should be fostered.
- An annual school of missions is conducted jointly with the commission on missions.

Finance.

- Understanding of the relationship between giving and the Christian life.
- Definite education in the Christian use of money.
- Promotion of the tithe and proportionate giving.
- Cultivation of special causes.
- Co-operation in the financial objectives of the church as a whole.

Christian social concerns.

- Familiarity with and application of the social creed of the churches.
- Encouragement of social service teaching and action.

170

- Guidance concerning Christian attitudes toward world order and international peace.
- Education in temperance and public morals.
- Guidance concerning interracial problems.

14. *Understands proper utilization of space and equipment.*
Guides in the wise assignment of rooms and equipment. Solves overcrowding by:
   - wiser use of space
   - multiple use of space
   - building more space
   - organizing outpost schools.

15. *Insures the keeping of adequate records.*
Supervises the use of the denominationally approved church-school record system. Works through the general secretary, insuring the making of all required reports.

16. *Undertakes faithfully the accomplishment of the three great imperatives which face every church school.*
   - *Improve quality of work done.*
   The whole organization and program of the school should continually be guided in the direction of improvement. Most of the items in this job analysis are for this purpose. This is one of the three great jobs of the church-school superintendent.
   - *Increase membership and attendance.*
   A church school that is not growing in members and attendance is dying. The membership cultivation superintendent is the officer who, under the administration of the church-school superintendent, is directly responsible. To see that the school grows in membership and attendance is the second great job of the church-school superintendent.
   - *Expand by organizing outposts.*
   In almost every section of the nation there is need for more church schools. Local church schools (working with the district superintendent) should start outpost schools wherever possible. This is the third great job of the church-school superintendent.

17. *Sees to it that youth and young adults are faced with the opportunities for service in full-time church vocations.*
Christian education leads naturally to Christian commitment and service. The church-school superintendent should be alert to guide proper youth and young adults into full-time vocational service to

the Master, such as the ministry, mission field, director of Christian education, minister of music, and the like. The superintendent should be a member of the committee on Christian vocations.

18. *Aids the commission on education in evaluating progress in procedures and in results.*

Helpful procedures:

Certain procedures will aid in achieving desired results. A school is proceeding effectively if it incorporates the following in an intelligent and adequate degree:

- adequate program
- proper literature and materials
- good teaching methods
- appropriate organization
- adequate leadership
- provision for increase and expansion
- adequate housing and equipment
- home and church-school co-operation

Desired results:

The effectiveness of a church school can be measured only by the results it is getting. If the answer to these questions is "yes," and in satisfactory measure, the results are effective.

- Are you helping people know God through Christ?
- Are you winning people to Christ and church membership?
- Are you developing habits of worship and use of the Bible?
- Are you producing persons for church vocations?
- Are you achieving Christian use of money?
- Are you growing in church-school membership and attendance?
- Are you developing service habits and helping community betterment?
- Are you establishing habits of church attendance and participation in the church program?
- Are you developing Christian homes?

The General Secretary

A secretary should:

1. *Understand that his work is vitally important.*
    - There is a direct connection between the work of the general secretary and the efficiency of the church school. If the general secretary proceeds with thoroughness, ways are opened for a good quality of work throughout the school, and for increases

in membership and attendance. This job analysis provides a quick summary of his duties.

- The general secretary should secure for himself and for all department secretaries detailed descriptive material explaining the use of the denominationally approved church-school record system.

2. *Understand the organization of the church school.*
  - Know the scope and organization of his own school.
    Whether the school is small or large, the secretary should know its structure thoroughly. The general secretary is more than a Sunday-school secretary. His work covers the whole church school.
  - Understand what a complete church school is.
    Understand the four parts of a modern church school, as follow:
    Sunday School
    Sunday Evening Fellowship
    Weekday Activities
    Home and Extension Program

3. *Keep up with progress and changes throughout the school.*
  - Know when classes or groups are newly started or discontinued so that provision can be made in the records of the school.
  - Know which classes or groups are increasing or diminishing in membership and attendance and inform the membership cultivation superintendent.
    One of the most important responsibilities of the general secretary is to co-operate closely with the membership cultivation superintendent, keeping him continually informed concerning gain or loss in membership and attendance.
  - Observe need for changes and improvements in the work of secretaries throughout the school.
    Inadequacies in the work of department, class, or group secretaries are often revealed in the records of the general secretary. Friendly assistance should be given in understanding how to make correction when necessary.

4. *Render service through membership in the commission on education.*
  - Keep the commission informed concerning the progress of the school as revealed by the records.
    The general secretary is the best source the commission on education has for information on the growth of the school.

173

- Enrich his own contribution as an individual commission member through his knowledge of the school.

5. *Serve as a leader of the secretaries throughout the school.*
    - Hold occasional meetings of secretaries to discuss responsibilities and problems.

        Such meetings, if conducted democratically and in a constructive spirit, can improve secretarial work throughout the school.

    - Counsel with individual secretaries concerning their work as may be desirable.

        Proceeding in a spirit of friendly helpfulness, suggestions can be brought to individual secretaries.

6. *See that minutes and records are kept, as may be advisable, throughout the school.*
    - Suggest the keeping of minutes of the commission on education and of the workers' conference.

        Be available for this service if asked. It may, however, be preferred to have a separate recording secretary for each of these responsibilities.

    - Suggest to the superintendent and to other administrators the preservation of important data for the permanent archives of the school.

        Information of permanent importance often is lost because no one assumes responsibility for its preservation.

    - Be responsible for the preservation of the basic records of the school.

        It is the duty of the general secretary to preserve permanently all the basic records of the school.

7. *Supply information to church and church-school leaders as may be requested.*
    - Constantly study the records of the school.

        Serve as a source from which other leaders secure information.

    - Be ready to interpret what the records reveal in order to assist leaders on request.

        Be able to indicate trends and interpret facts.

8. *Understand and supervise the use of the church-school record system.*
    - Know thoroughly the church-school record system in all its details.

        If possible, have a sample of each item in the system.

- Understand its purposes and how it should be used.

    This knowledge can be gained by a careful study of the available descriptive material.
- Aid the secretaries throughout the school in understanding and using the system.

    Discuss occasionally the entire record system in a meeting of all secretaries throughout the school. Each secretary should understand the parts of the system which he uses, and how the whole fits together.

9. *Co-operate with the church-school treasurer.*

    The division of responsibility between the secretary and the treasurer is not the same in all church schools. In some schools the secretary receives and records all offerings and then turns them over to the treasurer, either in cash or by depositing them in the bank for the treasurer. In other schools the treasurer assumes more responsibility. In any event, these two officers must co-operate closely.

10. *Be responsible for adequate membership rolls in the church school.*
    - Maintain the *central* roll.

        A central roll of members is recommended for all church schools, small or large. This is the duty of the general secretary.
    - Guide department, class, and group secretaries in maintaining their *working rolls.*

        The distinction between central roll and working rolls should be clear. Each secretary throughout the school should understand how to keep his working roll and to co-operate with the general secretary in keeping the central roll.

11. *Keep the records of the church school.*

    There are five types of records for which the general secretary should assume responsibility:

    membership records
    attendance records
    financial records
    progress records
    archives

    The first three, above, are automatically kept if the church-school record system is properly used. Progress records will show up in the records and minutes of the commission on education and of the workers' conference as the general secretary reports from time to time. Archives are the records, data, and objects which will have future value and which are preserved in some safe place.

12. *Be responsible for the making of reports throughout the school.*
   - Receive and post the weekly reports from departments and classes.

      This is a basic requirement. The general records are posted from the weekly reports.
   - Make reports as required.

      The general secretary is directly responsible for certain reports as stated below.
   - Assist others with their reports.

The General Treasurer

The general treasurer:

1. *Receives* all money brought to the general secretary for recording (not including amounts retained by classes, departments, or groups). This may be in the form of cash turned over to him or in the form of a bank deposit slip evidencing bank deposit made to the church school's account.

2. *Banks* all money for which he is responsible in a separate account in the name of the church school in a bank approved by the commission on education. This should be an invariable rule except in remote sections without banking facilities.

3. *Disburses* church-school funds by check only and only in accordance with policy of the church school regulating approval of disbursements.

4. *Accounts* for all funds entrusted to him:
   - by keeping his cash account in balance with bank statements
   - by maintaining accurate entries in the treasurer's book
   - by making all his records and check books available to church-school and church officials needing access to them
   - by submitting to an annual audit by the commission on finance.

5. *Proceeds* in all matters in accordance with the financial policy of the church school as developed by the commission on education.

6. *Is bonded* if the commission on education determines it to be in accordance with good financial policy.

7. *Is familiar* with the financial policy of the church school as determined by the commission on education. (See Chap. VIII and especially the form of financial policy statement beginning on p. 134).

176

8. *Is available* for consultation in financial matters by the commission on education and by church-school officials, without assuming a "watchdog" role.

The Church-School Librarian

It is for each local church to decide whether:

—The library should be operated under the commission on education by the church school for the benefit of the whole church, all organizations in the church having full opportunity to use its services. (This is recommended. A library is necessarily associated with education and the church school is its largest user, but other organizations can profit by its use.)

—Or whether the library should be operated under the official board in consultation with the commission on education and church-school leaders as well as in consultation with other users. (This is a workable plan, but it is cumbersome. If used, the official board should set up a representative library committee and should recognize the predominant position of the church school.)

—Or whether the library should be a church-school affair only. (This is not recommended in usual cases.)

This job analysis follows the first plan above. If another plan is used, adaptations can be made accordingly.

The librarian should:

1. *Understand that he works under the commission on education* to serve the church school and all other church organizations needing library service.

   • Library policy is determined by the commission on education in the interest of all users. The librarian should have access to the commission, attending and taking part in commission meetings when necessary to represent library interests.

   • The commission on education serves as a strong sponsoring body for the library. It is essential to the success of the library that it have such an anchorage in the organized life of the church.

   • In the commission on education, library matters would be the concern of the standing committee on lesson materials and teaching procedures.

2. *Maintain a teamwork relationship to church-school leaders.*

   • The church-school superintendent is the administrative officer of the commission on education and of the church school. The

177

librarian, as one of the general officers of the church school, works under his general supervision.

- Close working relationship should also be maintained by the librarian with all other leaders, division and department heads, teachers, counselors, leaders of groups.
- An occasional meeting is wise when the librarian and church-school leaders can discuss ways in which library services can be improved and expanded and utilization increased.
- A good librarian is alert to the value of good public relations. Friendliness is indispensable.

3. *Understand the purposes of a library.*
- To make available reference books and materials for teachers and other leaders.
- To make possible a reading service for shut-ins.
- To provide leisure-time reading for all within the field of the church and its broad interests. A church library does not attempt to duplicate the services of a general public library, but it does interpret its field broadly enough to encourage wholesome, cultural reading as well as reading in the field of religion. In setting policy for the library, the commission on education is wise in taking this into consideration. Services available from other libraries will be a factor in determining the scope of a church library.
- To serve as a depository for such records and archives as can appropriately be kept in a library. For instance, there should be a section on church-school records where general records of former years are kept permanently, not to be taken out but available for information and research.
- To provide storage and custody for current stocks of curriculum literature awaiting distribution to teachers and leaders. (Not all schools will want this arrangement. It often proves an efficient plan, however.)
- To maintain working files of back issues of church-school curriculum and periodical materials for research and reference.
- To maintain, for the use of administrators, teachers, and workers throughout the school, a file of the leaflets and booklets issued by the general board of education on the operation of a church school.

4. *Have a working knowledge of the library guidance literature of the church.*

Contact your general board of education for pamphlets and book-

178

lets on church-school libraries. These should be secured and mastered by the librarian.

5. *Know the church-school curriculum.*
   * Be familiar with the contents of the lesson material used throughout the church school.
   * Study ways in which items in the library could help teachers and leaders with their current preparation.
   * Maintain a close working relationship with teachers and leaders to learn their needs and to be in position to offer specific help from the library.

6. *Know the library.*
   It is a basic necessity that the librarian know what is in the library. This should be true both as to titles of items and as to general contents. The librarian is custodian of the library to be sure, but he is much more than that. He should be a competent guide to the user who needs to know how the library can help him.

7. *Maintain the library.*
   * Protect it against loss. Books are valuable property intrinsically, but a good library is valuable far beyond its dollar price. And if it is the depository of records, it can be priceless. That the librarian is a guardian does not mean that protection will be emphasized to the detriment of use.
   * Keep it clean and orderly. A disorderly library is discouraging and inexcusable and will fall into disuse. Order and cleanliness make use possible.
   * Arrange for replacement and expansion. Regardless of whether you have a large library budget, a small budget, or little or no budget, way must be found to replace worn-out books and to keep the library abreast of the growing needs of a growing church school. The commission on education is responsible for devising adequate policy in this respect.

8. *Know how to purchase books and library supplies.*
   The securing of books and other items for the library should be a carefully planned and guided matter. The commission on education should establish policy concerning the way in which books are to be added, especially relating to:
   * limitations on acceptance of donated books
   * procedure for selecting books to be purchased or accepted (This will involve expression of judgment from groups the library serves.)
   * amount to be invested annually in new and replacement books

179

These suggestions are pertinent: *Select* rather than *collect* books. Be acquainted with good books. Select books that are wanted and will be used. Provide for variety. Consider the activities and needs of those the library serves. Co-operate with other local libraries.

9. *Prepare books for circulation.*

It is a responsibility of the librarian to prepare new books for circulation. More is involved than simply putting them on the shelves of the library.

10. *Classify books as to subject matter.*

Dewey's classification method is recommended.

11. *Advertise the library.*

- Make use of bulletin board.
- Announce new books in church bulletin.
- Make attractive posters.
- With the approval and co-operation of their church-school leaders, have a story hour for children.
- Talk to small groups as to the importance of the library.
- Have "Open House."
- At workers' conference bring information about the library.

12. *Report periodically.*

Once a quarter submit a written report to the commission on education covering usage, condition, needs, budget expenditures, and recommendations.

The Person Who Orders Literature

1. *Know the church-school curriculum literature.*
   - Study descriptive material explaining the nature and purpose of each publication.
   - Become familiar with those publications which are used in the church school.
   - Be alert for wrong selection of literature and know the corrective.

2. *Understand that the commission on education is responsible for selecting curriculum material and that all literature orders are subject to its approval.*

3. *Understand the reasons for using denominational literature:*
   - They are:
     —It is planned and produced by and for the denomination.
     —It is based on the denominational point of view.
     —It undergirds a definite program of action.
     —It is subject to denominational direction and supervision.

—It creates loyalty to the denomination.
 * Be available to give this information to others when requested.
4. *Be prepared to advise with the commission on education.*
 * Know what is now being ordered and for whom.
 * Have in mind any recommendations for appropriate changes and additions.
 * Invite directions from the commission in furthering his work.
5. *Understand the working relationships in the church school.*
 * The commission on education is the authoritative body which decides what curriculum literature shall be used. The one who orders the literature carries out decisions but does not decide what literature shall be ordered.
 * The church-school superintendent is the administrative officer of the commission, and the one who orders the literature works under the superintendent (as do all other officers in the school).
 * Tactfully refer to the superintendent, for the attention of the commission on education, requests from teachers or others that literature other than that authorized by the commission on education be ordered for them.
 * Division and department superintendents often are given discretionary power by the commission on education to handle detailed decisions within general policy developed by the commission. In such cases the one ordering the literature works with them.
6. *Know and follow the plans of the denominational publisher in connection with ordering literature.*
 * Understand the order blank, how it is secured, procedures in filling it out, authorizations required.
 * Understand the time schedule in ordering literature—the specific time each quarter when the order should be mailed to insure having the literature when needed.
7. *Insure satisfactory distribution of the literature when received.*
 * Have it sent to the right address.
 * Arrange for the care of the packages as received.
 * Check incoming literature with order. Report discrepancies to the shipper.
 * Indicate to the proper person that the material has been received so that invoices may be approved and paid.
 * Have an adequate plan for distributing the literature.
 * Have a suitable place to store extra copies for which there may be later use.

181

8. *Be alert to avoid waste.*
- Study the quantity of each periodical actually needed to meet requirements safely but avoid waste.
- Make recommendations to the church-school superintendent accordingly, but do not change quantities ordered without authorization.
- Insure the gathering up of current literature left in the rooms and its return where extra copies are kept.

9. *Dispose of old literature.*
- Do not let it accumulate in scattered places throughout the building.
- Advise with the church-school superintendent concerning advantageous disposal, such as:
  —sending to some group which could make use of it
  —selling as waste paper
  —otherwise disposing of it.

An Analysis of the Pastor's Relationship to His Church School(s)

What responsibility does the pastor have for his church school (s) ?
In actual practice what attitudes do pastors take? Here are some samples. Which is best?

"I was called to preach the gospel and win souls to Christ. The church school is the business of the laymen. I prefer that they run it."

"If you want things done, you'd better do them yourself. In my churches I take active charge of the church school and see that it operates properly."

"I try to be pastor of my whole church. Everything related to my church is my responsibility, but I don't 'run' anything. I work through others. Today's pastor must be more than a preacher. Much of his work is done in ways other than preaching."

What interpretation is to be placed on the idea that nothing should be allowed to interfere with the pastor's authority and responsibility?

How does the pastor meet his responsibility for his church school (s) ?
Would the following be an acceptable analysis of the pastor's part?
He understands the basic function of the church school.
He insures the selection of competent leaders.
He guides those leaders as may be needed.
He maintains spiritual tone, morale, and enthusiasm.

1. *Understands the basic function of the church school.*
Would the following be acceptable as its function?
"The basic purpose of a church school is to help achieve the purposes of the church, using the teaching method. The job for the church school is to teach all for which the church stands."
Or this?
"The church school exists to do one magnificent thing—to teach the gospel."
Or this?
"The church in action as teacher is called the church school."
Or this?
"The church maintains its teaching branch (the church school) to provide the guidance people of all ages need to accept Christ as Savior and Lord and to live every day according to his teaching."

2. *Insures the selection of competent leaders.*
Would this be an acceptable approach?
—In the commission on education, have a person or a committee responsible for leadership.
—Through this committee and the commission itself, develop a long-range plan for solving the teacher and leader problems of the church school.
The plan would undertake to handle:
Discovery of persons to become leaders.
Enlistment of these prospects into the jobs needing them.
Training of all teachers and officers—new and old.
Maintenance of the staff at a high level of efficiency.
The plan could be organized around these ideas:
Have leadership standards.
Know leadership needs.
Select leaders wisely.
Enlist leaders intelligently.
Train leaders thoroughly.
Develop leaders constantly.
Correct misfits promptly.
Support leaders wholeheartedly.
As a companion to the plan of securing the best possible leadership, could the pastor then adopt the plan of giving great responsibility to these leaders? This would free the pastor for duties laymen cannot perform and would build sturdiness into the school.

3. *Guides those leaders as may be needed.*

• Is it practical for the pastor to talk with each new teacher or officer
—about the general purposes of the church school?
—about relating the church school to the church as a whole?
—about the skills required in the new job?
—about the deep satisfactions of serving in the church?
Or is all this the responsibility of the church-school superintendent or the chairman of the leadership committee? What is best?

• Should it not be a rule that the pastor *always* meets with the commission on education and the workers' conference, unless unavoidably prevented,
—to encourage by his presence?
—to enter into deliberations without dominating them?
—to guide in policy making if that becomes necessary?
—to inform concerning the total church program?
—to enlist co-operation of the church school in other phases of the church's work?

• Is it wise for the pastor himself to conduct annually a school to teach teachers to be personal evangelists in order to promote evangelism through the church school?

• Can the pastor wisely spend time, regularly, with the church-school superintendent, the chairman of the commission on education, and the director or minister of Christian education (where there is one)? A fine working relationship between these leaders is certainly very desirable.

• Should a portion of the pastor's pastoral visiting be directed to the workers in the church school, particularly where guidance or counsel is necessary?

• To what extent should the pastor himself be expected to possess the skills needed by teachers and officers
—in interpreting the basic purposes of Christian education?
—in guiding a teacher's development through reading?
—in interpreting the lesson materials?
—in developing good teaching methods?
—in stimulating increases in membership and attendance?
—in teaching the Christian use of time and money?

• If desirable, how can he acquire these skills if he does not have them?

• Can a pastor be expected to master

—the basic pamphlets on organization, administration, and method in the church school?

—the lesson materials to the extent of knowing from personal contact their tone, direction, and value?

—the general church-school periodicals?

- On what grounds can the pastor insist that only denominational lesson materials be used?

- What is the place of prayer in the whole matter? A pastor has many duties and his heart is often burdened. How much of his spiritual vitality can a pastor direct toward his church school? Of how much worth in the Kingdom is the church school?

4. *Maintains spiritual tone, morale, and enthusiasm.*

- To what extent is this actually the responsibility of the pastor?

—Does he undertake to carry this whole load?

—Or does he assume his share and supplement the efforts of other leaders?

- Who dreams the dreams—of growth in numbers and effectiveness, and of expansion to "possess the land"? Is this, too, a shared matter?

- How can a pastor, month after month and year after year, promote loyalty, encourage progress, build morale?

—How much of the load can the pulpit carry? Sermons on Christian education, friendly and encouraging references to fine work being done, enthusiastic announcements?

—How to conduct an effective installation service each fall for all teachers and officers? What are some good procedures to be followed? And some bad ones to be avoided?

—How express appreciation for services being rendered? An annual dinner by the commission on education, or the official board—with all teachers and workers guests of the church?

—How to reward unusual merit without favoritism or neglect of others whose quiet work goes unnoticed?

—letter writing

—pastoral visits

—phone calls

—general expressions of appreciation of attitude without naming individuals

- Who makes the church school a friendly place? To what extent is the pastor responsible for this? How can friendliness be promoted? Hospitality?

185

index